Blueprint
for a
Golden Society

By J.S. Boehme

ISBN-10: 1475181892
EAN-13: 9781475181890

Library of Congress Control Number: 2012906633
CreateSpace, North Charleston, SC

Cover graphic design by Leland Mark
www.spiritedbebop.wordpress.com

Cover art by Jason Christiansen
www.jasonsart.com

To Sandy —

Keep Being Yourself!

Much Love,

Jeff

*This blueprint is dedicated to my 6.5 billion sisters
and brothers presently incarnated on Earth.*

*May it help guide you to a Golden Future
and your rightful heritage.*

TABLE OF CONTENTS

Dedication		v
Table of Contents		vii
Acknowledgements		viii
Preface		xi
Introduction		1
1.	Why a Golden Society?	3
2.	Unlimited Free Energy	9
3.	Unlimited Clean Water	17
4.	Organic Whole Food	23
5.	Wellness Care for All	29
6.	Monetary Reform	43
7.	Universal Education	51
8.	Ending Poverty Forever	69
9.	Tax and Budget Reform	77
10.	The Golden Economy	89
11.	Free vs Fair Market	107
12.	Drug Policy	113
13.	Crime and Punishment	117
14.	Military and Foreign Policy	125
15.	World Unity Government	137
16.	Political Reform	141
17.	New Technologies	157
18.	The Celestial Neighborhood	163
19.	What Can I Do?	169
Author's Note		193

Acknowledgements

To Mom, who has always been there for me.
To Dad, who tried his best to teach an untamable child.
To Tracy, may you find and live your happiness.
To Amanda Panda, my Pumpkin Pie. Always be Amanda.
To Ella Bella, my Jelly Bean. Always be Ella.

To Penny Kay, sister of my heart, it's been a long strange trip indeed!
To Sunyata, brother of my soul, what do I say to the man with whom I need no words to speak? Is that the Light at the end of the tunnel... or a train coming our way?!!
To Pele-ma, you are always in my heart, no matter how far you are or how long it has been.
To Judith, thank you for sharing your wisdom with the world and your love with me.
To Sebastian and Vincent, thanks for showing me there are others out there as mischievous as me!
To Eliza, for having the courage to stand her ground in life after life.
To Bob, I wish things had worked out differently, and hope they still do.

To Bruce, from whom I learned so much, though we don't always see eye to eye.
To Steven, thank you for being a fine mentor. I hope your time wasn't wasted.
To Moses Yao, who helped me reconnect to the Earth.
To Malachais, wherever you are. When you initiated me on this path in Key West so long ago, did you have any idea how it would turn out?

And finally, in the place of honor, to Judy, without whose love and support I don't know how this book would have manifested.

Publishing Acknowledgements

For their assistance with proofreading, my thanks to Dr. Keri Ames, Ph.D., Dr. Judy Scher, D.C. and Louise Boehme.

For her assistance, advice and encouragement in the publishing process, and for being an overall ray of sunshine, many thanks to Jeraldine Peterson-Mark.

For his creativity and diligence in the design of the cover and interior images, thanks to Leland Mark.

There are far too many people who have influenced my life to list them all on these pages. Please forgive me if your name does not appear here. Know that you have my eternal Love and gratitude.

"The Fremen were supreme in that quality that the ancients called 'spannungsbogen' -which is the self-imposed delay between desire for a thing and the act of reaching out to grasp that thing."

FROM *DUNE*, BY FRANK HERBERT

Since I was a child of eight or so, I knew that life on Earth was not the way it was supposed to be. Nothing seemed right and it was very frustrating to a child growing up without the means to effectively address the situation. Since my teenage years, my entire life has been a search to discover Life's true purpose, to understand why things are the way they are, and to figure out a way to set things right. I tried to leave no stone unturned as I explored politics, economics, science, the military, human nature, spirituality, metaphysics and meditation.

As my meditation practice yielded results, I began to perceive reality very differently. I understood then that the answers I sought resided more in the higher realms of consciousness than the intellectual. Only by shifting our collective awareness will real change take place.

I sought my answers for the sake of my own understanding. I never desired to be a teacher, but those who shared teachings with me insisted that I share them with others. Throughout my adult life, even while continuing my personal exploration and learning process, I quietly conducted classes in advanced esoteric meditation for those who aspired. It has been an honor to share with so many brilliant beings.

My deepest drive, though, has always been to find a way to address the human condition on a global scale. Over the past decade, I attempted on multiple occasions to write this book. But, there were always more lessons to learn and greater awarenesses to attain. The time is finally here. This book represents the accumulated Wisdom of my life's quest and comes as much from the bloody noses as from the triumphs.

Together, we can create an indescribably beautiful future for all of humanity. This potential is very real. The political infighting and religious dogma must be dropped, and our minds must open to unprecedented possibilities, but there is a way. This is not some pie-in-the-sky, new age, airy fairy idealism. This blueprint is a very practical plan to use existing technology and logistical skills to harness the energy of Creation and move with the flow of Nature to create a better life for ourselves, for our children and for every future generation.

The greatest challenge will be to release our preconceptions in order to change our way of thinking and move into a new paradigm of interaction with each other, with ourselves and with Life. Isn't it ironic that one of the most difficult challenges in life isn't a doing, but a letting go? You can't leave on the ship while you are holding on to the dock. Let go of who you think you are so you can find the real You.

This is an exciting time to be alive! Great changes are upon us. If we come together now, the world we create will earn the gratitude of all future generations.

J. S. Boehme
Santa Fe, NM
April 10, 2012

"I cannot tune a harp or play a lyre, but I can make a great State from a small city."

-THEMISTOCLES

"You've got to be very careful if you don't know where you are going, because you might not get there."

-YOGI BERRA

"Poo-tee-weet"

-KURT VONNEGUT, JR.

INTRODUCTION

We live in a Cosmos of infinite energy and highly organized diversity. Harmony is the natural order. Abundance is our natural state. Creating a harmonious society in which each person leads an enriching, fulfilling life is so simple, so easy that it seems surreal that this book needs to be written. All of our problems can be solved simply by organizing our society in accord with the Laws of Nature and the Flow of Life.

Creating a harmonious society can be likened to floating downstream in a canoe. Working in concert with the flow of energy that is present, there is almost no effort involved. Left to its own devices, the canoe would float down the river and out to sea. It just happens. There is no need to ply a paddle except to avoid an obstacle, to speed toward the goal, or for the sheer joy of paddling. The same is true if we join in the Flow of Life. With a little conscious guidance and effort, our society will arrive at a place of harmony, fulfillment and abundance for all.

For things to have become this chaotic, this disharmonious, there had to be a deliberate, organized effort. The dysfunction of our current situation can be likened to forcing the canoe upstream. The effort to move upstream is difficult and tiresome, sapping energy and strength, taking a huge amount of constant effort. It took a conscious choice and organized effort to convince humanity to paddle upstream, particularly when one realizes that the goal of life, in this analogy, is to reach the mouth of the river and the ocean of harmony, fulfillment and abundance that lies beyond.

There presently exists a large body of excellent research investigating the whos, hows and whys behind the deliberate creation of the current societal dysfunction. Many informative documentaries, books and websites detail that data. I encourage you to explore them at your leisure. There is no need to repeat that work here. My purpose is to present solutions. If humanity collectively applies these solutions, the whos, hows and whys will fade into the background of the blooming of a vibrant, thriving future for all humankind.

As with Nature, the solutions are elegant in their simplicity, yet as intertwined as a complex symphony in which each chord adds to the harmony of the Whole. These solutions are meant to be seen as integral elements of an integrated entity, each strand affecting the entire web. As with any interdependent system, eliminating individual elements would have significant effects on the balance and harmony of the remainder.

Humanity has reached a crossroads. Our defining moment is upon us. Open your heart and mind to new ways of doing Life and an exhilarating adventure will unfold before you. A glorious future awaits. All that is required is a choice. Bon voyage! Enjoy the journey!

"What senses do we lack that we cannot see and cannot hear another world all around us?"

FROM *DUNE*, BY FRANK HERBERT

To create a society in harmony with Life, the purpose of Life must first be understood. A society is a microcosm of Creation. Societal structure is a reflection of a society's conception of the macrocosm. A false concept results in a flawed society. *"As above, so below"* states the Hermetic maxim. To create a harmonious structure below, we must first understand that which is above.

The ills of modern society are the direct result of a flawed, antiquated, artificially manufactured belief in what is above. A dualistic perspective prevails, expressed as Good vs Evil and the associated idea of Heaven and Hell. Current social structure reflects this duality, manifesting in many ways: Christian vs Muslim, White vs Black, East vs West, Communism vs Capitalism, Republican vs Democrat. It always boils down to some form of Good vs Evil. The irony is that both sides see themselves as Good and their opponents as Evil. It would be comic if it weren't so tragic.

THE MEANING OF LIFE

The purpose of Life must be understood in order to create a harmonious society. It is more simple than you might think: Life is a school. You may even think of it as a 'Universe-ity.' Everything in it is alive and exists to learn, grow and increase in complexity.

Anything that has a magnetic field is alive and has awareness, though its life and awareness may be far different from the human

3

concept of those terms. Everything that is alive is on an individual path of growth. Humans simply have not developed the external technology, nor, other than a few rare individuals, the internal awareness to perceive this truth or to communicate with most forms of life.

Everything is alive, from simple hydrogen atoms to universes filled with billions of galaxies. Each being is a student in the School of Life and is undergoing the same process of experience, growth, change and expansion. Just as a child in kindergarten is in the same school system as a Ph.D. candidate, atoms and universes are simply in different grades in the School of Life. As a being becomes more complex, so does its consciousness. If you think some humans are complex, consider the consciousness of a star... a galaxy... a universe!

Life is eternal, but everything has a life cycle. Universes and galaxies are born in Big Bangs, expand and grow, and eventually come to an end. Stars are born, ignite, become sources of energy and light, complete a life cycle, then supernova, sending their constituent elements with their individual awarenesses out into the galaxy to combine with other elements from other stars to form new celestial bodies with new experiences and new learnings. The awarenesses of those beings are far beyond our current ability to even imagine.

In reality, the term 'life cycle' refers to the life container, the body housing the consciousness of the being. Life cycles pertain to celestial bodies as surely as human bodies. Consciousness never dies. It just changes containers. If consciousness were to be stuck in one container for eternity, its learning and growth potential would be capped and Life's purpose would be foiled. Thus, eventually, the container is destroyed and the consciousness moves on.

Death is just a transition from one learning vehicle to another. If the Life lessons were learned well enough by the time the transition comes, consciousness can move on to a more complex form of life, allowing for a new range of lessons. This process is quite analogous to being promoted to the next grade in school or being detained, depending on how well the required course material was learned.

When an individual comes to understand the purpose of Life, it can then begin to concentrate on learning Life's true lessons. The focus changes from acquisition of wealth, power, status, and the other distractions of a dualistic society, to personal growth and expansion of awareness.

A Golden Society understands that Life is a school and that every being is a student. It therefore seeks to embed itself harmoniously in Life by creating a culture that reflects that reality. It provides the infrastructure and resources for its citizens to learn and grow. A Golden Society understands that as each member attains his or her individual growth and fulfillment, society as a whole moves closer to peace and harmony with the Whole.

A Golden Society is a society of the heart. It is in the heart that the true essence of every human being resides. That which makes us bubble inside, which brings us joy and passion, is who we are. We are what we Love. By this, I don't mean what we desire or what we lust after. Those are weak joys, if joys at all. I am referring to the unconditional, infinitely powerful Universal Love which is inside each of us.

Life is a school. Pain and joy are its teachers. Life ideally tries to teach us through joy. It is when we ignore the messages of joy that pain is invoked. Life will invoke as much pain as necessary to teach the needed lesson. Life prefers to use the carrot, but it will use the stick. Once this principle is understood, beings naturally move toward the reward and away from the punishment.

When we learn to listen to and follow the joy, life becomes a beautiful, happy, fulfilling adventure. The heart is the residence of that Joy and Love. By following our hearts, we follow the path of Love to our True Selves. It is the ingenious design of Creation to use Love to guide us to higher awareness and true fulfillment.

Sadly, many religions have fallen to the point that they teach the reverse of this Truth. They insist that suffering and pain are holy and that joy and pleasure are sinful. Hence, they drive their adherents ever farther from their True Selves and Divine Natures.

Think about it: what kind of deity would create a world in which suffering is beneficial and in which our innermost drives toward joy and pleasure are really traps to ensnare us? What kind of being would create a world in which we are supposed to follow the stick and run away from the carrot? That seems more like divine sadism than the acts of a just and loving god.

The Love within our hearts is the guide to our True Essence. Our heart is our internal GPS. It is not only our right, but our duty as human beings to follow this Love to the places it leads. By doing so, we embed ourselves into the harmonious flow of Creation and fulfill the divine purpose of our existence.

The greatest violation that can be done to other beings is preventing them from following this Love and being themselves. Yet, the governments and religions of today do exactly that.

The seminal essence of every true religion and mystical system comes down to one simple message: Be YourSelf. It is that simple. Any time that any religious, political or societal message deviates from that Truth, you can be certain that they have lost their way and fallen into illusion and falsehood.

The purpose of a Golden Society is to provide the support, freedom and resources for the individual citizens to follow their hearts, to embody their Love, and to discover their True Essence through working toward fulfillment and self-actualization.

Having the right and duty to follow your heart and Be YourSelf is not a license for laxness. It does not mean the right to do what you feel like or be what you want. It means discipline, focus, work and effort. If your heart tells you to be an Olympic sprinter, you absolutely have that right and duty. No one has the right to tell you differently or to try to force you to be a doctor, a lawyer or anything else. Yet, following the call of your heart puts a great responsibility on you.

Being an Olympic sprinter requires an enormous amount of effort and discipline. A specific diet must be followed, a training regimen must be adhered, sleep must be regulated, alcohol and drugs eliminated. Following the heart allows ultimate freedom, but it requires great self-control.

Many people who are not ready to accept this level of personal responsibility surrender their personal power and are easily led astray. For many, it is easier to believe someone else than it is to do the Work necessary to Know and to be responsible for themselves.

Work is part of the lesson plan. Individual growth is attained as much from the regimen required to achieve a goal as from the joy experienced from its pursuit and the fulfillment derived from its achievement. Life is the greatest teacher. The heart shows the way. A Golden Society provides the support system.

WHY IS IT GOLDEN?

"*"As above, so below."* I call this a Golden Society because of its relationship to the corresponding realms of Creation. About midway between the third dimension in which we live and the One Light, which is sometimes called the Crown Chakra of the Cosmos, exist the Eternal Golden Regions. These Realms are composed entirely of self-luminous Golden Light. Many religions associate these Golden Regions with Heaven. Since the experience there is of all-encompassing, Universal Love, this association is understandable. The concept that the streets of Heaven are paved with gold comes from these Regions. The uninitiated do not understand that the 'streets of gold' actually refer to Golden Light.

I am convinced that these Realms of Eternal Golden Light are the Heart Chakra of the Cosmos. *"As above, so below."* As the Golden Realms exist midway between the Earth and the Crown of the Cosmos, so the heart exists midway between the root and the crown of a human. A Golden Society, a society based in the heart, is the temporal counterpart of these Golden Regions of Creation, an expression of Universal Love on the Earthly level.

The heart sees the Unity of all Life. A Golden Society knows the interconnected nature of all of Creation and understands that what happens to one strand affects the entire web. Therefore, a Golden Society looks to the wellness of the Whole, understanding its effect on each individual, and simultaneously looks to the wellness of each individual, understanding the effect on the Whole.

A Golden Society also is aware of its place in the grand scheme of things. It understands its role in the School of Life and conducts itself accordingly. A Golden Society is aware of that which is above and seeks consciously to replicate it below.

Being heart-based, a Golden Society does not promote profit motive or the accumulation of material wealth and temporal power as ends unto themselves. There is nothing inherently wrong with material wealth and possessions, but a Golden Society understands that these are transient, insubstantial and of no real value when it comes time to change life containers. Material wealth in a Golden Society is merely a means to an end.

Part of the beauty of a Golden Society is that, because it functions in harmony with the Laws of Nature, abundance is available to all. It is ironic that there will be greater material wealth in a Golden Society than in the present materially focused culture.

Only experience, awareness and wisdom can be taken along when it is time to drop your body and move on. A Golden Society understands that these constitute the true wealth of Life and are the only riches that can accompany us on our eternal journey.

Thus, a Golden Society promotes quality of life, joy, love, fulfillment, learning, growth and wisdom. These are the qualities that will advance students to the next grade in the School of Life. Thus, when it is fully understood that Life is a school whose purpose is learning and growth, it is a simple matter to arrange society to support this purpose.

A societal infrastructure that supports its citizens to achieve healthy lifestyles, to meet their individual material needs easily, and to achieve their educational goals while promoting freedom of thought and freedom of expression will create a fulfilled, flourishing populace. With the creative potential of the population set free, the people will continuously develop new ways to meet the needs of society while promoting an ever expanding growth and fulfillment curve. With an understanding of the heart-based nature of human existence, a Golden Society logically follows.

There will always be more to learn and more growth to attain. One day, humanity will be ready to transition to a Silver Society and a new Blueprint will be given. First, we must firmly establish ourselves in our hearts. One must learn to walk before one can run.

Chapter 2
Unlimited Free Energy

Free energy has been available to humanity since the time of Nikola Tesla, who proposed to connect to 'the very wheelwork of Nature.' He was in the process of building an antenna tower that would broadcast energy waves long distances. Eventually, this system was to cover the globe so every person could tune in to unlimited, nonpolluting free energy as simply as tuning a radio to a particular station.

Since the early 1900s, there has been no need for oil, gas, coal, nuclear, hydro or any other conventional means of power production. Tesla's discovery clearly threatened the power of the energy cartel. Seeing there would be no more power transmission lines, J.P. Morgan uttered his famous quote, *"Where can I put the meter?"*

Shortly thereafter, Tesla's funding was discontinued and the project was abandoned. Tesla eventually died alone and destitute with his dream unrealized. Upon his death, his research was seized by government agents and hidden from the public. Since Tesla's time, dozens of inventors have developed multiple free energy devices and water powered cars. Each of these inventors has been subjected to various forms of intimidation and suppression. Many have met untimely, often violent deaths under suspicious circumstances.

Thankfully, the internet provides a means for information distribution that is difficult to control totally. Investigate for yourself. Simple searches for free energy, overunity, electrostatic motors and other related topics return an amazing amount of information in video and written form. Understanding the infinite power of Creation and the amount of energy radiating from a Big Bang, it is no surprise that human ingenuity has found a way to tap into this infinite creative source. The surprise is how effectively it has been suppressed... until now.

THE PRICE WE HAVE PAID

The reasons for suppression should be obvious. Not only is energy a multi-trillion dollar annual cash cow, there is great political power to be had by controlling a commodity needed by everyone. The energy cartel is not only taking your money. It is sucking your energy and your life through the time it takes you to earn the money to purchase a product that is infinitely plentiful and should be free.

The current energy industry also brings grave health, environmental and social costs. Think of all the environmental damage and human suffering caused by the energy industry over the past century.

Remember Chernobyl, Three Mile Island and the radiation leak caused by the earthquake and tsunami that hit Japan. How many people in the last century have died prematurely or lived with extreme health issues caused by radioactive pollutants?

Depleted uranium shells are used by the military in an effort to find a secondary market for radioactive waste. Cancer rates of children living in the deserts of Iraq near battlefields where these shells have been used are significantly higher than prior to the wars.

Tons of radioactive waste have to be transported through populated areas, then stored for hundreds of thousands of years. Our radioactive legacy will exist longer than the entirety of known human history.

Remember the Exxon Valdez spill, the catastrophe on the Deepwater Horizon drilling platform and the countless other oil spills on land and at sea. Uncounted animal and plant life have been killed. The environment and the food supply have suffered drastic contamination. Genetic structures of many species have been degraded.

Think about the dangers inherent in the production and use of combustible fuels. How many people have been horribly maimed or killed in gasoline and other fuel explosions?

Air pollution from coal and oil power plants, combustion engines and even wood smoke affect billions indiscriminately. Consider how over half of the children living in some highly polluted urban areas have lesions in their lungs. Think about the children in Calcutta, Beijing and other cities whose air quality standards are even looser than in the U.S. Acid rain also damages the environment and pollutes the water supply. Entire forests are dying from acid rain damage.

Consider the environmental and social impact of rivers dammed to create hydroelectric power. More than five million Chinese may ultimately be displaced by the construction of the Three Gorges Dam.

While energy profits run in the trillions each year, poverty stricken people in third world villages don't have the means to pump water for drinking, bathing or irrigation and don't have electricity to light their homes. How much money and quality of life has been needlessly sucked from families around the globe?

The list is egregious, but it must be faced. The price paid for the energy industry's greed and hunger for power goes far beyond dollars and cents. None of this harm was necessary. The destructiveness can end today through the widespread introduction of technology that already exists. We have the solution in our hands.

TRIPPING OVER OUR OWN FEET

Sadly enough, some of the inventors of free energy devices are hampering introduction of the technology. Desire for secrecy to prevent patent infringement has caused some inventors to keep information to themselves. With the data thus centralized, the energy cartel can easily suppress an invention by eliminating only one person.

Other inventors charge exorbitant prices in an effort to match the profit level of the energy cartel. Some will only rent or lease their inventions in an effort to maintain a monopoly on the technology. Still others hold back their inventions, awaiting fairy tale billionaire benefactors to drop millions in their lap for mass production. Many inventors don't seem to understand that the people with

11

the most have the most to lose, and that potential benefactors can be frightened away by the threats of the energy establishment.

Many of the minds with the mechanical and electrical genius to create free energy lack the strategic and organizational intelligence to get their inventions through the gauntlet and into the hands of the public. An inventor with a functioning, scalable prototype could introduce his product to the public in a grass roots way that would require little capital and be difficult to suppress. He or she would have to be willing to settle for a modest profit and the satisfaction of being one of humanity's great benefactors, but it can be done. Such an inventor is welcome to contact me.

It would be fantastic to see a completely altruistic inventor post on the internet open source plans to build free energy devices. Such plans, posted on thousands of websites in dozens of countries would be very difficult to suppress. Disseminating the information so widely would empower the public and protect the inventor from the intimidation and threats of the energy cartel.

THE SOLAR/WIND DISTRACTION

I hate to rain on the parade of many well intentioned environmentalists, but solar and wind power are allowed by the establishment as distractions to keep the populace from focusing on real solutions. Yes, clean power can be obtained from solar, wind, tide and other sources. But, these are expensive and yield comparatively little power per dollar invested. There have been recent improvements in solar power that produce far greater yields than before, but it still doesn't compare to free energy power production.

By influencing the populace to concentrate on solutions that are impracticable in the long term, the energy establishment keeps the focus away from the real danger to their monopoly. Free energy devices are comparatively inexpensive to build, scalable, portable and are not dependent on weather conditions or time of day. They work constantly and continuously in virtually any condition to power homes, factories, vehicles, equipment, appliances and they even work in outer space.

I celebrate the spirit of altruism, activism and inventiveness shown by solar and wind power proponents, but I encourage them to rethink their positions. It would be better to focus that energy and creativity on a more comprehensive and functional solution. Stop allowing the establishment to use your good intentions to manipulate and control you. Free energy is the solution from which they are distracting you with the sleight of hand of solar and wind power.

THE GOOD NEWS

The good news is that free energy devices are real and already exist in many forms. We only need to find the collective will to mass produce and distribute them. In a Golden Society, free energy for all will be a priority. With our current manufacturing and logistical capacities, every person on Earth can have access to unlimited free energy in a matter of a few years.

Imagine the benefits of unlimited free energy for all. Imagine a world with no air or water pollution, with no nuclear waste, with only small dams for drinking water and irrigation reservoirs. Small villages in Africa, Asia and around the globe will have light and fresh water where there never was any before.

Imagine independence from a collective power grid. In the event of a natural or man made disaster, those not directly affected will have uninterrupted access to power. Those who are directly effected can be supplied with reserve power devices and brought back online within hours or days. Never again will a cascade reaction leave millions without power. No more blackouts or brownouts or downed power lines.

Imagine owning homes, vehicles and appliances fitted with their own energy sources. Without the friction of combustion engines, wear on vehicles and other devices will be drastically reduced. Imagine purchasing only one vehicle in your entire life, a vehicle which needs only minimal maintenance and never needs to be replaced.

Now consider the direct savings free energy will have in your life. Add up the money you spend annually on gasoline or diesel along with oil changes for your vehicle. Combine that sum with the amount you spend on electricity, natural gas, propane and other forms of energy used in your home. If you really want to be thorough, add the cost of the batteries in your automobiles, appliances, toys, and flashlights. This is how much you will directly save every year of your life.

Now, look at indirect savings. Think about the energy costs to manufacture a product and to light the factory. Think about the fuel costs to ship the product from overseas or to freight it over land via truck or train. Think about how much of the price of a plane ticket or the price of shipping an overnight package goes to fuel expense.

Consider the farm equipment needed to grow and harvest your food, the pumps for irrigation, the heat for greenhouses. Think about the fuel for shipping from farm to warehouse to grocery store. Think about the refrigeration to keep perishables cold.

50% to 90% of the retail cost of most goods is the energy cost of production and transportation. This includes groceries and agricultural products. Even at the low end of that scale, the effect on your life is significant.

Even if your income does not change one jot, you will have more than twice the spending power you had prior to free energy. When monetary and other reforms that are part of a Golden Society take effect, you will have even more. How will your life look different if you have twice the money available? Or three times? Or even more? Would you buy healthier food? Better health care? Improve your living conditions? Work less? Vacation more? Take time to work on a special project? Go back to school? Spend time with family?

Free energy production will also create an entirely new economic sector that will more than make up for any jobs lost in the discontinuation of the old energy industry. There will be careers building, installing and maintaining free energy devices, and there will be research and development positions involved with improving and advancing existing technologies.

The psychological and spiritual ramifications of free energy will be profound as well. Right now, there is a mass psychology of dependence on central authority. The current system imprints the concept that we lack the resources to be independent and that we must apply to our superiors and pay a price for energy. In a Golden Society, each citizen will have access to unlimited energy. Individual energy independence on a material level will create a psychology of emotional, mental and spiritual independence.

Free energy is here. It is a reality. It is how Nature works. A universe doesn't go to a gas station in order to create a Big Bang. A galaxy doesn't go to the power company to create a black hole. The system currently in place goes against the design of Nature and, consequently, it is destined to collapse at some point.

Free energy is our right. It is our birthright. It is part of Nature. Free energy can and should be a basis for a new societal structure, a new consciousness of the infinite plentitude of absolute abundance. Free energy is a key to an entirely new way of viewing our world. We must demand our right, gather our collective will and assert that which is ours. The possibilities are endless.

CHAPTER 3
UNLIMITED CLEAN WATER

We live on a planet that is over two-thirds water. Yet, according to the World Water Council, over 1.1 billion people lack access to clean water. That is one out of every six people.

Desertification claims over 20,000 square miles of land each year, rendering agricultural land unusable and natural habitat unlivable. Populations are suffering from food shortages due to drought and lack of irrigation.

Free energy technology empowers a revolutionary solution, literally. Over half of the human population lives less than 200 miles from a coastline. 44% live within 100 miles. Advanced desalination and pumping technology is already in use in many countries. The only barrier to mass desalination and widespread distribution of fresh water is the expense of the intense energy the process requires.

With free energy technology, we can produce virtually limitless quantities of fresh water with no danger and no pollution. Excess salt can be safely redistributed in the ocean. Tests have shown that there is no adverse effect as long as the discharge is minimally dispersed. There is currently more than adequate technology to do this and the technology will advance and improve over time.

Part of the beauty of this solution is the minimal danger. If a fresh water pipe breaks, so what? Instead of an oil spill, there is only a fresh water spill whether on land or in the sea. If a discharge pipe breaks, salt water is temporarily discharged undersea in a higher concentration. There is no negative environmental impact in either case.

With over half of the population living within 200 miles of the sea, the fresh water needs of the entire coastal population can be provided by desalination. We have the technology to pump water much farther than 200 miles, but we can use this distance for our practical calculations. With coastal needs met through desalination, demand for water from inland sources will be reduced by over one half, reducing the strain on rivers, lakes, aquifers and other fresh water sources.

Offshore oil rig technology can be adapted to fresh water production. Floating desalinization plants can be built at central manufacturing sites and then towed to their production sites. In this manner, third world countries and isolated locations can be supplied as easily as first world.

There are multiple additional advantages to these floating fresh water rigs. Offshore platforms can be staggered and separated to more effectively disperse the saline discharge. In the event of natural or man made disaster, relief platforms can be towed to disaster areas to provide quantities of fresh water almost instantly.

The environmental benefits are manyfold. Inland lakes and reservoirs can be refilled and new ones can be created. Standing water seeps through the soil and replenishes the aquifers, providing water for any who dig a well in the area. This can actually extend the desalinated fresh water supply far beyond 200 miles from the coast as water in aquifers can migrate much farther inland.

In addition to providing ample fresh water for drinking, cooking, sanitation and hygiene, there will also be water for irrigation and habitat reclamation. The food supply can be increased greatly and food prices will drop as areas that were once considered arid and unfarmable become vibrant farmland.

There is a myth that the current population level is too high and there are too many people for the planet to sustain. This perception is absolutely untrue. A more accurate statement would be, "There are too many people on the planet to be sustained using current methods and practices."

If every person on the planet went to Australia, there would be a quarter of an acre of land for each person with 10% of Australia left over along with all of the remaining land masses on the planet. There is plenty of space on the planet if used wisely. With free energy, desalinization and sustainable farming and manufacturing, there are ample resources for everyone on the planet to live abundant, fulfilling lives.

There are vast swaths of land once rich with vegetation and diverse ecosystems that have been desertified through poor farming practices, overgrazing and clear cut logging. Environmental organizations, often working in concert with cooperative governments, have yielded amazing results in habitat reclamation.

Through introduction of native species, terracing to prevent erosion, and controlled grazing, huge expanses of land in China, Africa and elsewhere have been reclaimed. Living soil, humus, has returned. This humus traps and filters rain water, allowing the soil to remain moist for extended periods of time, irrigating plants naturally. Rivers now run clear rather than murky with silt from soil erosion and run off.

Aquifers that were once dry have refilled, making well water available again. Lands that had become completely barren are now rich with natural vegetation. Crop yields are many times what they were prior to the reclamation. If these projects have been able to accomplish so much using only the fresh water available through rainfall, how much more can be accomplished with an influx of fresh, desalinated water?

The potential for countering global warming is extremely exciting as well. Yes, it has been shown that not all global warming is caused by man. Some of it is caused by cycles of solar flares and other natural factors. Regardless of the causes, the impact can be minimized through working with the Earth's natural systems enhanced by desalinated water.

Increasing vegetation cover, particularly trees, reduces surface temperature. Biomass sequesters carbon. The living humus actually stores up to four times more carbon than the living plants themselves. Vast quantities of water are also stored in the biomass.

More fresh water can be stored in refilled inland lakes, reservoirs and and depleted aquifers. Fresh water stored on land and trapped in biomass is an effective counter to potential rises in ocean level due to melting polar caps. With reduction in surface temperatures, the melting ice caps themselves may even be restored.

With more water stored in biomass and inland bodies, subsequent increased evaporation will increase rainfall and shift weather patterns, providing fresh water to areas that haven't seen rain for some time. Nature already has the technology to counter global warming. We just need to work with that technology and enhance it using desalinated water.

Free energy not only provides the means to desalinate and pump the water, it also provides the means to power heavy equipment used in terracing, building reservoirs and other tasks involved in habitat reclamation. All of these solutions tie together to enhance one another, just as the web of life in an ecosystem works together to create balance and harmony for all. These solutions are in harmony with and use Nature as a model, as it should be.

Another positive effect of habitat reclamation is increased atmospheric oxygen. Currently oxygen levels on the planet have fallen to between 20% and 21% and continue to drop with the burning of fossil fuels and the reduction of biomass. 19.5% is considered oxygen deficient for humans and can cause loss of consciousness and death.

With free energy replacing fossil fuel technology, carbon dioxide emissions will fall to the lowest level since man began lighting fires for cooking and warmth. Couple that with the increased photosynthetic oxygen production from greater biomass, and atmospheric oxygen levels will increase. This will have many beneficial effects.

Many diseases including cancer are anaerobic and cannot survive in high oxygen environments. Brain function increases with higher blood oxygen levels. Many yogic breathing techniques are designed to increase oxygen levels to activate higher brain function and associated expanded awareness. Imagine the effect a higher atmospheric oxygen content will have on human consciousness.

Another benefit of creating this desalinized fresh water network is the opening of an entirely new economic sector. There will be jobs and business opportunities in manufacturing, installing and operating desalinization plants and pumping stations as well as opportunities in research and development. There will also be entirely new business and employment opportunities in the new sector of habitat reclamation as well as in manufacturing specialized equipment designed for that field. Work will also be available in irrigation and water distribution along with the creation and maintenance of new reservoirs and man made lakes. There will be more family farms and agricultural employment as arid land is made arable.

In short, the creation of abundant fresh water through desalinization using free energy is a win-win-win-win situation. It will, directly and indirectly, be a boon to every person on this planet and it will allow a Golden Society to embed harmoniously into the natural order while providing abundance for all.

CHAPTER 4
ORGANIC WHOLE FOOD

Food is such a basic, fundamental part of human existence that the need to write this chapter blows my mind. The food supply has become polluted, debased and devoid of nutrition. There are actual poisons in some foods and some of the foods themselves are poisons. This is allowed, even encouraged and subsidized, in the name of profit. Don't get me wrong. I have nothing against making an honest profit. But, that profit should be honest and should not come at the expense of human life and quality of life.

Social control is another motive for manipulation of the food supply. That can easily be researched on your own. There is a plethora of data available. Here, we will focus on solutions.

Fortunately, the solution is, like so many others, extremely simple. The degraded food supply can be solved with three words: Organics, Humane Husbandry.

If all of our food is grown organically, then the harmful elements will be removed. There will be no more genetically modified organisms, hormones, or chemical pesticides, herbicides and fertilizers. Not only will the harmful elements be removed, but the food itself will become more rich with life and nutrients. There are more than enough advanced organic farming techniques to replace conventional chemical methods with minimal or no loss of yield.

Even with slightly lower yields, profits for farmers will increase due to decreased expenses. Working with Nature by using natural means of fertilization, pest control and weed control is far less expensive than paying for their petroleum based counterparts. Couple those savings with the savings from using farm equipment powered by free energy, and the cost of food will decrease significantly even as quality rises. Organic whole foods under this system will cost less than half of current prices while providing greater nutrition, health benefits and quality of life.

I am going to include drinking water here as part of the food supply. Currently, the U.S. is one of the few remaining countries that fluoridate the drinking water. Fluoride is a poison and is known to cause brain damage and other adverse health effects. It has no real proven benefit for dental health when added to drinking water.

Some researchers hypothesize that fluoride is used to make the population docile. During World War II, Russia used it in the gulags and Germany used it in the stalags to keep their prison populations under control. Regardless of the reasons for its addition to our water supply, it is time to discontinue its use. Doing so will improve health while saving money.

As quality of life and general health increase, disease will decrease. This in and of itself will be a benefit to society, but there will also be indirect financial benefits in the forms of reduced health care costs as well as increased productivity thanks to lower health related absenteeism.

We will also benefit globally from the restoration of living soil. Humus is far different than dirt. Dirt is just dirt. Humus is a living, breathing ecosystem. Living soil contains countless life forms, from beneficial microbes and fungi to insects and earthworms. Humus retains water, requiring less fresh water for irrigation. It also allows the excess water to filter into the aquifer rather than run off carrying away topsoil and silt into our river system.

We have already discussed how living soil sequesters up to four times the amount of carbon than living plants. This carbon remains in the living soil even after the plants have been harvested. Imagine the effect on global warming if living soil is returned to all current and future farmland. It takes a few years to rebuild humus, but the long term benefits are self-evident.

Chemical pesticides, herbicides and fertilizers kill the soil. They leave behind only barren dirt, which has little to no nutritional value for the plants, erodes easily, and has comparatively minimal water retention. Dirt has simply become a medium into which chemical fertilizers can be injected to be absorbed by the plants to give the appearance of life and health. This contaminated, lifeless dirt also creates a pollution nightmare.

Agricultural runoff is one of the most prevalent forms of water pollution today. Dirt and silt clog streams and rivers. Toxic fertilizers, herbicides and pesticides pollute the water supply. These chemicals flow into the river system and seep into the ground water, polluting the aquifers. Human breast milk has been shown to retain large quantities of these chemicals, passing on toxins to our infants when their bodies are in their most vulnerable formative stages.

Another form of agricultural pollution that few people consider is the massive manure run off from the huge industrial animal factories. This is, in essence, allowing raw sewage to run into our river system and water supply. In an organic based farming system that works with Nature's functioning systems, this manure would be collected, composted and turned into fertilizer to enhance the living soil and increase production.

This brings us to humane husbandry. The cruel, heartless ways in which the meat and dairy industries raise animals is unconscionable. Animals are packed into tight spaces without the ability to move, standing and sleeping in their own urine and feces. They are injected with and fed antibiotics to fight the diseases that are prevalent from the unsanitary, unnatural conditions. They are fed hormones to speed growth and fed chemically raised grains. In many cases, the animals that succumb to disease are ground up and fed back to the other animals in the factory farm.

Did you know that grain is poisonous to cattle? If you feed a cow nothing but grain, it will die in a matter of months. But, since grain fattens cattle and causes fast growth, these industrial farms play a game. They feed the cattle as much grain as they can with the goal of butchering them just prior to their dying from grain poisoning. Does anyone actually believe that meat from a diseased and poisoned dying animal is healthy to eat?

This is all done for the sake of profit motive without any consideration given to the cruelty to the animals or the health detriment to the public. An entire book could be written on this subject, and, indeed, many have along with some excellent documentaries. I encourage you to research this on your own.

Animal husbandry needs to go back to that, husbandry, the breeding and ***caring for animals***. Why are there laws preventing cruelty to pets, but not to livestock? All animals raised for meat, dairy, eggs and clothing fiber should be allowed free range, healthy living conditions and be fed a diet consistent with their natural requirements. Yes, this will cause the prices of these commodities to increase, but the market will balance based on the true demand for these products versus other forms of protein and minerals such as beans and other legumes.

Here is some data that points to the social control side of this issue. Did you know that 74% of government food subsidies go to meat and dairy? 13% go to grains, most of which are feed grains that go to the meat and dairy industries. 11% go to sugar, oil, starch and alcohol. Less than one half of one percent of agricultural subsidies go to fruits and vegetables. These numbers are completely contrary to the FDA's own recommendation for a healthy, balanced diet. Why are the least healthy components of our diet being given the most financial subsidy?

Don't get me wrong. I am not against meat. Everything in moderation (including moderation!) is one of my mottos. I grew up on a cattle ranch and we raised and butchered other animals as well, but they were free range and grass fed. I still enjoy a good steak, though I choose organic, free range whenever possible.

I do object to cruelty and inhumane treatment of animals. I object to meat that is filled with hormones and antibiotics and fed an unhealthy diet. And, I object to financial manipulation of the market to increase consumption of certain dietary elements to unhealthy levels. Right now, it is cheaper to buy a fast food burger with all of its ill effects than it is to buy a salad or an equal portion of fruit. Think about it.

Imagine being able to go into any food establishment anywhere, whether it is a fast food franchise or the local grocery store, and know that everything you buy is organically grown and all of the meat is humanely raised. If all food had to meet the same organic and humane standards, then there would be a level playing field for all, from the small family owned farm to the agribusiness conglomerate, from the fast food franchise to the fine dining restaurant. Without subsidies and artificial price manipulation, demand for healthier foods will cause shifts in production to meet that demand.

Agribusiness corporations have long since learned that a relatively small amount of money donated to the right campaigns can net tens of millions in subsidies and price supports and innumerable laws biased in their favor. This political influence has put agribusiness corporations at the head of an effort to drive out small farmers and consolidate all food production under the umbrella of a few large businesses.

Family farms are attacked through financial manipulation, patenting seed, efforts to have organic food illegalized as unsafe, and making it illegal for farmers to store and use their own seed. Unbelievably, Congress is participating in this process in exchange for a relatively small amount of money in the campaign coffers.

An alarming sign of the disharmony of our current agricultural system is the disappearance of the honey bees. Entire colonies disappear without a trace. This phenomena has been labeled Colony Collapse Disorder and has filled the scientific community with consternation for several years. Science demonstrates that if the all bees disappear from the Earth, all life will be affected within a few years. Plants need bees to pollinate and reproduce. Without those plants, there will be a huge gap in the food chain and all other life will suffer dramatically if not die out entirely.

Until recently, scientists have been baffled by Colony Collapse Disorder. Now, there is evidence that it is due to systemic pesticides, herbicides and fertilizers. Systemic means they are absorbed into the plant and permeate its systems. Bees have been filmed landing on plants treated with systemic chemicals. After collecting pollen, the bees take off, fly in irregular patterns and ultimately fall to the ground and die.

Europe has already banned systemic chemicals, but with Congress in the pocket of agribusiness, the United States has yet to do so. How amazing that these politicians and business people would rather chance permanent ecological destruction rather than reduce short term profits.

I have observed that many people have an inherent joy in working the land and working with animals. This trait seems to be a fundamental part of human nature. I believe that no matter how technologically advanced humans become, there will always be a segment of the population that thrives from digging their hands in the soil and causing things to grow.

Even now, there is a movement from urban areas back to rural. Professionals are quitting their careers, moving to the country and buying small farms and ranches. They are finding great peace and joy working the land and working with animals. These people are a significant part of the growing trend toward sustainable, natural agriculture.

As the playing field becomes balanced and the undue influence of large corporations is removed, there will be a movement back to small family owned farms. Family farming will once again become a significant sector of our economy. People will make comfortable incomes and live fulfilling lives while providing nutritious, delicious, healthy and plentiful food.

The solution is so simple that the need to write it still seems surreal. Three little words that bring so many benefits on so many levels: Organics, Humane Husbandry. The benefits include improved nutrition, better health, higher quality of life, decreased pollution, return of the living soil, carbon sequestration, lower food costs, reduced water use, happier and healthier livestock, and sustainable and fair economic growth.

Organic whole food is one integral strand in the web of a Golden Society. It affects and is affected by each part of that web. The whole cannot be considered without the parts, nor the parts without the whole.

Health care is another human need so basic, so fundamental that it should go without saying. Not only is it a moral and ethical imperative, universal health care makes financial sense and, most importantly, supports the achievement of Life's purpose. Understanding that Life is about learning and growth, it logically follows that a healthy population is more capable of achieving those ends.

Here, we will refer to wellness care rather than health care. Wellness care emphasizes maintaining optimal health and well being while preventing disease and illness. In its current usage, health care carries connotations of repairing damage and fixing problems after they occur.

PROFIT OVER HEALTH

Unfortunately, the current health care system is based on profit rather than healing. This is one of the most heartless elements of the current socioeconomic system. Consideration for the well being of individuals and society as a whole is discarded or overruled in favor of a twisted economic logic.

The baseline assumption is that economic growth is good for everyone. The medical sector is a huge portion of the overall economy. Therefore, growth of the medical industry driven by demand for health care is considered an economic boon. Based on this perverse logic, the more people who are sick or injured, the sicker they are, the longer they remain sick and the more often they get sick, the healthier the economy will be and the better off we are. By this reasoning, water pollution, air pollution and food contaminants are beneficial, because they drive the medical-health care sector of the economic engine.

The 'profit over health' ethic ignores cures and even suppresses them if they are not sufficiently profitable. For example, because current laws prevent natural substances from being patented, they are not as profitable as synthetic treatments. Consequently, pharmaceutical companies ignore effective natural cures outright or actively suppress them. Those who discover and promote natural cures are threatened, attacked violently and even killed.

The cancer industry in the U.S. alone grossed over $100 Billion in 2010. In 2009, total medical spending topped $2.5 Trillion. This amount of money is more than enough to encourage underhanded tactics by corporate profiteers. Wars have been started for far less.

As with agribusiness, large pharmaceutical companies make significant campaign donations. Consequently, laws are enacted that favor these corporations over patients. In the 2010 elections, over $31 Million was donated by the pharmaceutical industry to campaigns through direct donations, PACs and soft money.

In return, these corporations, in effect, get to write the medical and insurance laws and dictate to the FDA. Natural cures that work but don't profit the large corporations are made illegal, don't receive FDA approval and are not covered in the U.S. by private insurance, Medicare, or Medicaid.

Most doctors, nurses and other medical professionals that I have met are extremely competent, kind, caring individuals. They have often expressed frustration with the current system, feeling their hands are tied by regulations and by the mercenary nature of the medical industry. They understand and chafe at the profit based motivations of many decisions and dictates of the health care establishment.

The ugly truth of the medical establishment went from theoretical to first hand knowledge for me in August of 2009 when my mother was diagnosed with lung cancer. The tumor was about the size of a tangerine and had just begun to metastasize. Her doctors basically wrote her off and expected her to go home to die. Being the person that she is, she took up the challenge and began researching the subject. Initially, she treated herself through diet. But, since the cancer was so advanced by the time it was diagnosed, she needed a more aggressive treatment.

She ruled out traditional chemotherapy because of the negative side effects. Her research yielded several effective treatment options. But, these treatments were not available in the U.S. since they were based all or in part on natural substances that couldn't be patented. Since these treatments were not FDA approved, Medicare and private insurance would not cover them. She had to go to Mexico to get treatment, and she had to pay for it herself.

The artificial boom and bust business cycle had already consumed a large portion of her retirement fund. She spent the remainder on cancer treatment. She even had to mortgage her house to pay for the most recent visit. But, after four trips to Mexican cancer clinics, she has outlived her original prognosis by over two years. Unfortunately, the stress of having her entire retirement consumed is having its own adverse affect on her health. Her attitude is outstanding, though: better to be alive and broke than dead and flush.

Unfortunately, this story is not unique to my mother and is all too common across the U.S. Now I can understand why medical bankruptcy is the number one form in the U.S. I can truly sympathize with those who are wiped out by health care costs. My parents did everything the 'right' way. They owned a business and worked hard and very long hours, far more than 40 per week. My mother was even an elected official on the local level for a time. My parents paid all their bills and taxes, saved and invested and prepared for retirement. Now my mother has no assets and only a small income from Social Security and her pension as an elected official. In the end, it turns out that she is only a cog in the economic machine and she is worth more to the establishment sick and broke than healthy and flush.

Fortunately, the solution for her and for everyone else is rather simple. Wellness care can be provided for all at lower cost with greater health and overall higher quality of life.

INTEGRATED APPROACH

Wellness is interrelated with policies already discussed in this book and others that will be discussed in future chapters. It cannot effectively be treated separately. Healthy, nutritious organic food and clean water will promote greater levels of health. Many of today's physical and psychological ailments are directly related to the common acidic, sugary, fatty, chemical laden diet and the many environmental pollutants.

Reduced pollution resulting from free energy and clean agriculture will result in greater levels of wellness. Education in diet, exercise and other techniques to maintain health will also contribute. As financial stressors are removed, general emotional and physical wellness will improve. As quality of life increases along with general happiness and fulfillment, overall well being will improve.

All of these factors that increase general health combine to directly reduce wellness care costs. An indirect savings for a healthier population comes from the productivity that will no longer be lost due to illness. From cancer alone in 2010, it is estimated that over $20 Billion of productivity was lost due to illness, and over $140 Billion of productivity was lost due to premature death. That totals over $160 Billion of lost productivity compared to $102 Billion in the direct costs of cancer treatment. A system that promotes wellness and health maintenance could pay for itself in productivity savings alone!

Eliminating the Profit Motive: Wellness will be maintained at a much higher level in a Golden Society, significantly reducing health care costs. Other factors will reduce costs even more and help pay for the remaining expenses.

Removing the profit motive from the medical industry will be a key to returning it to its purpose of caring for the health and wellness of the citizens. Once again, I want to emphasize that there is nothing inherently wrong with making an honest profit. But, it should not be done at the expense of human well being.

Because they are ruled by profit motive, insurance companies seek to minimize costs by excluding high risk individuals and individuals with preexisting conditions. They also seek to give minimum care to those in need. Many hospitals and clinics are also owned by for-profit corporations. Sadly, they seek to maximize profit from the pain and suffering of others.

There is an assumption in our current society that if there is no profit, people will not be motivated to do a good job. This simply is not true, particularly in a Golden Society. People coming from their hearts work in healing fields for the joy of helping others. Yes, they need to be remunerated for their time, effort and expertise. But, billions of dollars of profit do not need to be generated for the medical establishment to function with quality and efficiency.

CEOs should make decisions about hospital operations based on providing maximum quality wellness care rather than basing them on profitability and stock value. The medical industry can function with superior levels of quality and efficiency without profit as its primary motivator.

Rethinking Medical Insurance: In a Golden Society, medical insurance will be completely rethought. Insurance is based on spreading risk. Resources are pooled and used to pay for care for those who end up in need. For-profit insurance companies seek to reduce their risk and increase their profits by excluding higher risk segments of the population from the pool. This is logical if the purpose of insurance is to generate profit. It is not. **The purpose of wellness care insurance is to spread risk, ensuring that everyone has affordable access to wellness care.**

Universal Coverage: In a Golden Society, the first rule of medical insurance is *"Everyone is covered."* No one will be excluded regardless of risk, preexisting conditions or for any other reason. Including everyone makes the insurance pool equal to the population as a whole. Therefore, the risk factor is exactly the same for each organization that engages in the business of medical insurance. Such equity and impartiality is the quintessence of a level playing field and fair market competition.

Insurance Mutuals: The next solution already exists in the modern insurance industry: insurance mutuals. *An insurance mutual is a nonprofit insurance organization owned by its members*. Each member pays into the pool each year. Money remaining at the end of the year is returned to the members on a pro rata basis or held in a fund to pay future benefits.

I currently belong to an insurance mutual for my automobile insurance. It happens to be one of the finest companies I have had the pleasure of dealing with in any sector of the economy. It is run efficiently, professionally and courteously.

Members are encouraged to drive safely and otherwise to reduce individual expenses as a benefit to the whole. Each year, my share of any excess income is either invested by the mutual into a subscriber savings account as a hedge against future claims or returned in a refund check. This policy encourages responsible driving since the savings from reduced expenses directly benefit the members.

If this system works so well for auto, property and other insurance, why can't it work for wellness care? If multiple insurance mutuals operate on a level playing field, then they will compete for business by providing the best value at the best price. To reduce costs, they will be motivated to encourage higher levels of wellness through diet, exercise, health maintenance techniques and education. They will also police the pharmaceutical and medical establishments, preventing price gouging and fraud.

With the undue influence of pharmaceutical and medical lobbies removed, insurance mutuals will be open to alternative forms of treatment. Their focus will be on the most effective treatments rather than the most profitable. If a $5 natural remedy is equally or more effective than $50 in pharmaceuticals, then insurance mutuals will opt for the natural remedy. If a situation can be treated by a change in diet rather than a lifelong course of injections or pills, there will be motivation to encourage the dietary change even though it means less profit for the medical establishment.

Insurance mutuals would also pursue the cost effectiveness of promoting bodywork and other wellness therapies that increase well being and boost the immune system. Massage, Rolfing, cranial sacral and a host of other techniques that reduce stress and build wellness will be incorporated. As the adage goes, an ounce of prevention is worth a pound of cure.

TREAT THE DIS-EASE

By addressing the dis-ease rather than the symptoms, health and quality of life will be improved while long term costs are reduced. In modern medicine, often the symptoms are treated without seeking to address their root cause. Pain and other symptoms are often expressions of deeper imbalances. Through seeking and treating the root cause, equilibrium, wellness and optimal health are returned.

For example, often when someone goes to a doctor with back pain, a pain killer is prescribed and the patient is sent on his or her way. In actuality, the pain is a signal that there is a deeper issue that needs to be healed.

By simply blocking the pain symptom without addressing its source, the original condition is often exacerbated. The pain symptom increases and higher levels of pain medication are needed. This cycle can continue indefinitely until the dis-ease and resulting back pain becomes so severe that surgery is required. Accompanying the surgery is a hospital stay, antibiotics, rehab, lost productivity, more pain killers and a host of other expenses.

There is a cutting edge form of chiropractic called Network Spinal Analysis. Its focus is 'Reorganizational Healing' or assisting the body and being to access a state of wellness that is inherent within each of us. Rather than address the symptom of pain directly, Reorganizational Healing views the pain as a signal and a bearer of deeper wisdom and seeks to learn from it and to address the underlying cause. Network care will ultimately not only address the pain, but it will heal the source of the pain, assisting the body to optimal functionality, creating wellness in the entire being and improving quality of life.

In this example, let's say that 100 sessions of Network Spinal Analysis are needed at $40 per session. That $4000 is still far less than the direct costs of surgery and a lifetime of pain killing medications, not to mention the indirect costs of the progressive degradation of quality of life and functionality. Gaining the priceless state of optimal wellness will enhance the patient's life immeasurably.

Similarly, heartburn can be healed with dietary changes and reduced stress levels rather than just suppressing the symptoms with acid blocking pharmaceuticals. Most diabetes can be controlled with diet and lifestyle changes rather than the costly daily intake of insulin. Insurance mutuals in a Golden Society will understand this principle and will act for the benefit of their members.

THE GENERAL ASSISTANCE FUND (GAF)

The savings resulting from the institution of the above measures will greatly reduce the cost of wellness care insurance. With lower costs along with increased disposable income resulting from energy, monetary and other Golden reforms, wellness care insurance will immediately be within the financial reach of most of the population. Within one generation, it will be affordable for all.

I am a big believer in personal responsibility. But, I also believe in fairness and community. In life, each person is ultimately responsible for him or herself. Unfortunately, the deck is stacked against many people.

Societal resources are currently distributed in such a way that many citizens do not have the means to provide for themselves and their families. Access to obtaining these needed resources is systematically restricted by the very structure and function of modern society. A poverty mentality has been created, and a system of dependence has been instituted. Individuals have been robbed of their independence, self-worth and personal empowerment as a result of this institution.

In a Golden Society, poverty will be eliminated within one generation. Since poverty does currently exist, a solution will be needed to create a bridge to that goal. An assistance fund will provide that bridge, helping those whose incomes are below the poverty line.

Individual assistance accounts can be established for those in need. Money can then be loaned from the assistance fund to pay insurance premiums for those in poverty. The loan amount will accrue to the individual assistance accounts at no interest or at a low rate. With modern technology, tracking these loans will be a simple matter.

When individuals rise out of poverty, their assistance accounts can be repaid on a predetermined basis through garnishing a percentage of any marginal income above the poverty line. As loans are repaid, more funds will be available to assist others in need. When poverty is eventually eliminated, the loans will be fully repaid. The fund can then be redistributed to the population through refunds, used to reduce taxes or applied to other projects.

For example, if the poverty line is set at $20,000.00 per year, then individuals earning less than that amount will be eligible to borrow from the General Assistance Fund and will not be required to make payments. If their income rises to $30,000.00 in a particular year, then they will have to make payments based on a percentage of the marginal $10,000.00 earned above the poverty line. If the repayment rate is set at 50%, the repayment amount for that year will be $5000.00 and the individual will keep $25,000.00 of that year's earnings. If their income increases to $50,000.00, then the garnishment will be $15,000.00 and their retained income will be $35,000.00.

By garnishing only a percentage of the marginal income above poverty, people will still have incentive to earn more since they will be able to retain the balance for themselves. It will not take long for individuals who have moved out of poverty to repay any assistance funds they needed. When their assistance loans have been fully repaid, the borrowers will retain all future earnings for themselves.

Using this system, people will be free to choose their own insurance mutual just as if they were paying with their own funds. The only difference is that their premiums will be paid from the assistance fund. They will receive the same care and have the same options and choices that are available to the rest of the public. This is a fair and equitable means to help others to help themselves.

Other Benefits of the General Assistance Fund: A sizable portion of medical fees currently charged by hospitals are needed to cover the costs of medical treatments for those who cannot pay out of pocket and do not have insurance. This system is unfair to all.

Impoverished people who do not have medical insurance often have no choice but to go to the emergency room for treatment.

They are billed by the hospital at exorbitant emergency room rates for the treatment rendered. Since the patient cannot pay, the hospital transfers their bills to collection agencies who report the debt to credit bureaus. Credit records are ruined. Life becomes even more difficult for the poverty stricken. Renting a home becomes a challenge. Auto and other insurance rates rise and loans become practically impossible to obtain. The chances of climbing out of poverty are further reduced and the cycle perpetuates itself.

The hospitals must account for the losses incurred by providing services to those who cannot pay. Hospitals do this by charging more to those who can pay, unfairly shifting the burden through higher insurance rates and medical fees. Whether it is through taxes paid for a public insurance system or through higher rates in the current private system, those who pay for their own medical expenses end up paying for those who cannot.

Through creation of the General Assistance Fund (GAF), insurance rates will drop for all since each individual will only be responsible for his or her portion of the overall pool. The impoverished will be responsible for their debt to the GAF, but at a reasonable interest rate rather than the 18% or more charged by collection agencies and hospitals. Repayment will trigger automatically when their income rises above the poverty line. These debts will not have negative effects on credit ratings and thus will not be a barrier to upward movement through society.

Even if some people pass away without fully repaying their assistance loans, the Golden system is still far more cost effective than the current system which taxes for Medicare and Medicaid while leaving millions uninsured. Currently, the financial burden for medical care for the uninsured is unfairly shifted to other segments of the population.

HOSPITAL REFORM

Changing hospitals to nonprofit institutions will also reduce costs. Hospital administrators and medical personnel definitely should be paid competitive wages for the invaluable work they do. Yet, adding in profits for stockholders and hospital owners puts an unwarranted financial burden on patients and the insurance industry. The decision making process for hospital administrators should be focused on maximizing healing, not increasing profits.

The current establishment promotes the idea that profit motive maximizes efficiency. This fallacy has been proven false time and again. In fact, our current medical system is highly profitable, but it is ranked 37th in quality by the World Health Organization. Healers, as with all people in a Golden Society, choose their profession for the love of the work. As long as they are given fair compensation for their time and expertise, they will be happy to do their work. Their joy is the work itself and the satisfaction of helping others.

If capital investment is needed to build a hospital, it can be set up so the capital is repaid along with a one time fair return. The hospital can charge fair prices for its services with the surplus going to repay the investment. Upon full repayment, future surplus income can go to a capital fund to pay for future expansions, renovations and equipment upgrades, or it can be donated to the GAF or other funds to help the needy.

MALPRACTICE REFORM

Another cause of inflated medical costs is the malpractice system. Massive punitive damages are often rewarded in malpractice cases. Unfortunately, this does not effectively change the behavior of the medical professional or institution in question. Mostly, it punishes the public through higher prices. Malpractice insurance covers the damages leaving the culprit virtually unharmed. The associated high premiums are factored in to the cost charged to patients. Thus, the punitive damages don't really act as a disincentive to doctors or hospitals, but they do increase the medical costs of consumers.

If someone has suffered from malpractice, they certainly should be compensated. Medical treatment to correct the damage, if that is possible, should be provided. Lost work time, current and future, should be compensated. Loss of quality of life in the case of egregious situations should also be compensated to a point. But, huge punitive damages aimed at punishing an individual or institution should not be issued.

It would be far more effective to make the malpractice ruling easily accessible public knowledge and, in certain cases, to suspend or revoke the license of the professional or institution involved. It would be a rather simple and inexpensive matter to set up a searchable malpractice database. Convictions of malpractice would be recorded there.

When people are seeking new doctors or hospitals, it would be easy to research their malpractice history, directly affecting professionals' and institutions' ability to maintain their business and attract new clients. Easily accessible malpractice information provides strong incentive to act professionally and will have a much greater effect than the current malpractice system.

In the event of multiple convictions or an egregious conviction, a review board can choose to suspend a license or revoke it entirely. The review board can also require the offender to attend additional schooling in order to reinstate his or her license. This solution presents real consequences to medical professionals and institutions without increasing medical costs to the consumer.

WORKERS' COMPENSATION REFORM

Universal wellness care eliminates the need for workers' compensation insurance, a huge expense to businesses. I understand the reason for its creation, but workers' comp is a costly drain. Wage replacement insurance is beneficial, but workers end up needing and society ends up paying for two types of medical insurance, one for when they are at work and one for the rest of their lives. The beauty of this scam is that its costs are hidden from the general public. If each person had to pay for two types of insurance out of their own pocket, there would be a general rebellion. So, workers' comp is paid by the employer. But, the employers don't just pay for it. They raise prices to compensate for the expense. So, in the end, the general public pays for workers' comp as surely as if they paid for it directly out of their own pockets.

With wellness coverage for all, each person will be covered 100% of the time whether at home, work, vacation or the grocery store. There will be no need for secondary workers' compensation policies.

Once the insurance pool is spread among the entire population, the risk is managed equitably.

High risk industries may warrant higher insurance rates. For jobs such as firefighters and Alaska crab fishermen whose risk factors are far above the norm, employers would pay a surcharge on a per employee basis directly to the insurance mutuals chosen by the individual employees. Since these surcharges would be industry wide, competition would remain fair. The cost would be integrated into the price of the goods or services provided by those businesses. The employee would remain responsible for his or her own standard wellness care policy. The risk surcharge would be paid by the employer.

Such a system is a far more fair and economical means of managing the higher risk of those jobs than than having two separate insurance policies for every person in the work force. Employers will still have the responsibility of maintaining safe working environments. Negligence could result in fines, raised risk-surcharge rates, temporary suspensions and the closing of businesses.

AFTERWORD

Upon exposure to the facts, open minds will see that the for-profit system of the old medical paradigm does not work. Annual profits are hundreds of billions of dollars for medical corporations while millions of people go without insurance and proper medical care. People live with illness or die prematurely while viable cures are ignored and suppressed because they lack profitability. Meanwhile, the World Health Organization ranks the United States 37th in world health systems.

Wellness care and quality of life can be improved while reducing costs by:

- reducing pollution and environmental toxins
- improving the quality of the food and water supply
- increasing wellness education
- reducing the political influence of medical corporations
- allowing for 'alternative' treatments

- eliminating insurance exclusions for any reason
- insuring through nonprofit medical insurance mutuals
- making hospitals and other medical facilities nonprofit organizations
- providing a General Assistance Fund for the impoverished
- replacing punitive damages with a malpractice database
- eliminating workers' compensation insurance

In a Golden Society, a universal wellness care system will not only provide medical care for all. It will improve quality of care and well being while reducing costs. Providing wellness care for all is as simple as applying common sense, willpower and heart.

"*C*** *ontrol the coinage and the courts. Let the rabble have the rest."* I was about 14 years old when I first read that quote in *Dune*. At the time, I really had no idea what it meant, but now I can see what a man of vision and political savvy Frank Herbert truly was. He echoed the sentiment of private central bankers throughout history, including Mayer Anselm Rothschild who in the 18th Century said, *"Permit me to issue and control the money of the nation and I care not who makes its laws."*

He who controls the money supply controls political power. Shrewd manipulation of the money supply can cause booms and depressions, start wars and decide who wins them, raise and destroy monarchs and rig elections. Possibly the greatest deception of our time concerns the control and use of the money supply.

THE GREATEST SCAM OF ALL

When I studied financial management in college, I was indoctrinated with the party line that the Federal Reserve Board was appointed by the government, but was necessarily independent because politicians would be too tempted to print money to solve problems, causing inflation and instability. An independent body, so they said, was needed to keep the money supply safe from political manipulation. It was taught that the Federal Reserve was the part of the government charged with issuing the money supply, but was independent from executive and legislative control for that reason.

As with most good deceptions, the reality of the situation is completely contrary to the image presented. The Federal Reserve is an independent bank that has no Constitutional connection to the government. It is wholly owned by private stockholders, many of them foreign nationals. The Fed expands and contracts the money supply at its own behest and for its own benefit and it uses the money supply for political manipulation.

It is a stunning revelation to discover that our money is not money at all. It is debt. It is created as debt through loans to the government, the public, other banks and foreign nations. If all debt were paid off, there would be no money.

The Federal Reserve creates money out of thin air and loans it to the U.S. government and to other entities. National and local banks create money out of thin air and loan it to the public. This is the magic of fractional reserve banking.

Banks don't have to have money to loan money. They just need a fraction, usually 10% or less. In other words, a bank can loan 10 times (or whatever the current fractional reserve requirement) the amount it has in its vault. And get this: the money kept in its vault as reserve requirements was created as a loan in the first place, whether by the same or a different bank.

All of our money is debt, and it is all controlled by the Federal Reserve Bank. We merely exchange debt instruments and think we are spending money. The same holds true for private central banks in other countries.

The Federal Reserve manipulates the economy in two main ways. Primarily, it shrinks and expands the money supply through direct creation of money and through control of the fractional reserve requirement. If the Fed wants the money supply to grow, it lowers the requirement, allowing banks to create more loans/money from the same reserves in their vaults. If the Fed wants to shrink the money supply, it raises the reserve requirement, reducing the amount of loans/money banks can create from those same reserves. (I use the term 'vault' figuratively, as much of this money exists as ones and zeros in cyberspace.)

The second and better known means of manipulating the economy is through control of interest rates. If the Fed wants to slow the economy, it raises interest rates, reducing demand for loans. If it wants to accelerate the economy, it reduces interest rates, increasing demand for loans. Interest rates are not adjusted for the good of the public, but for the profit and power motives of the faceless stockholders of the Federal Reserve.

The bankers use the money supply in an insidious way to harvest wealth from the people. By increasing the money supply and providing easily obtained loans and lower interest rates, the economy moves into a boom phase. People are thus encouraged to borrow more to purchase property, vehicles, and equipment, to start businesses, and for a myriad of other purposes.

Then, the bankers contract the money supply. Often, higher interest rates accompany the contraction. Since there is less money available, the economy slows, spending decreases, and loans are defaulted. Real estate, businesses, equipment, vehicles and other property are foreclosed upon and become possessions of the banks.

Thus, by creating money out of thin air and by manipulating the money supply through controlling reserve requirements and interest rates, bankers are able to accumulate real property of real value without any real expenditures on their part. In this way, the people are fleeced of their wealth and the bankers are enriched in real terms.

One of the sad ironies is that, according to the reasoning used to justify its creation, this boom and bust pattern called the 'business cycle' is precisely what the Federal Reserve was founded to prevent. Yet, look at economic graphs beginning in 1913 with the creation of the Federal Reserve. You will find booms and busts with clock-like regularity.

MANIPULATING POLITICS

Despite popular impression, elected officials have virtually no control over the economy. In fact, the opposite is true. The economy controls them. If a President doesn't submit to the wishes of the Fed, it simply contracts the money supply, thus creating a recession or depression. The public blames the President and votes in a new one. The irony is that the new elected officials will have no more control over the economy than the last. Even sincere politicians are either forced to submit or be voted out of office. Politicians just present an illusion of control, ultimately acting as front men for the Fed.

The practice of using the money supply to manipulate politics goes back centuries prior to the founding of the United States. In fact, according to Benjamin Franklin, a major reason for the founding of the United States was to escape the manipulation of the money supply by European central banks. Other Founding Fathers echoed this sentiment. Sadly, the European private bankers have progressively insinuated themselves into the banking system of the United States until, ultimately, the Federal Reserve Act of 1913 ceded full power to them.

The truth is finally surfacing. There are fantastic documentaries and books available that delve into this subject. I invite you to educate yourself more fully on this vital matter. I cannot stress the importance of this issue enough. For now, suffice it to understand a few crucial points:

- The money supply is not issued or controlled in any way by the government or by the people's representatives.
- Money is debt. It is issued by private bankers who create it out of thin air and loan it either directly to the public or indirectly through loans to the government. Either way, it must be repaid with interest.

BENEFITS OF A GOVERNMENT ISSUED CURRENCY

If the government issued our currency, we would no longer be saddled by the national debt with its attendant interest expense. The tax burden would be significantly reduced without reducing public services. There would be price stability, inflation would be controlled, and citizens would retain their wealth.

Abraham Lincoln said, *"The government should create, issue and circulate all the currency and credit needed to satisfy the spending power of the government and the buying power of consumers..... The privilege of creating and issuing money is not only the supreme prerogative of Government, but it is the Government's greatest creative opportunity."*

The purpose of a money supply is to provide a medium of exchange for goods and services. If there is sufficient money, it is easy to do business. Without sufficient money, business becomes more difficult and the economy slows. If the money supply equals the size of the economy (the amount of goods and services available), prices remain stable. If the money supply grows faster than the economy, prices inflate. If the economy grows faster than the money supply, prices deflate.

For prices to remain stable, the money supply needs to grow at the same rate as the economy. As an example, say the economy is $7 Trillion and it grows by 5% in a year. At the end of that year, the economy will be $7.350 Trillion, 5% or $350 Billion larger than the previous year. For prices to remain stable, the money supply also needs to grow by $350 Billion. Under the current Federal Reserve controlled system, that $350 Billion is created as loans. Then, the $350 Billion *plus interest* has to be repaid to the banks.

Under a government issued money supply, the $350 Billion would be created by the government and spent into the economy. In other words, the government would use the newly created money to build bridges, educate children, send shuttles into space or on any of the myriad other government services.

For that year, the tax burden would be reduced by $350 Billion plus there would be no interest and no principle repayment. Everyone would benefit except for those few bank stockholders who stood to make $350 Billion plus interest by creating money out of thin air. It is for this reason that Lincoln referred to issuing currency as "... *the Government's greatest creative opportunity.*"

The above is a simplified example, but you should get the point. The economy and the money supply exist in ratio to one another. For prices to remain stable, the money supply and the economy need to grow in direct proportion. Increases in the money supply can either be created by the government to benefit the people, or by bankers to benefit bankers.

It is no wonder that these bankers guard their monopoly so jealously. They have the means to control the world with little or no effort on their part. It is simply a matter of clicking a mouse and typing in numbers. As long as the public accepts the illusion, the bankers remain in control, regardless of the political or economic system.

THE SOLUTION

Fortunately, as always, the solution is simple. Repeal the Federal Reserve Act and close the Federal Reserve. Allow *only* the government to issue currency. Replace existing Federal Reserve currency with government issued currency and require banks to maintain 100% reserves for their loans.

I had my own ideas about how to replace the Federal Reserve debt-based currency with government issued currency. Then, I heard the following plan originated by the economist Milton Friedman and promoted by the Money Masters. It parallels my idea, but goes a step further.

The national debt is roughly equivalent to the total debt based money supply. About 10% is issued directly by the Federal Reserve and used to buy government bonds. The remainder is issued through loans from private banks. In the Friedman/Money Masters plan, as the government issues its own currency, the new money is used to repay the national debt, thus replacing the Federal Reserve currency while simultaneously retiring the national debt and keeping the money supply stable.

When the national debt is fully retired, the burden of its interest will be removed. That will save the taxpayers around $400 Billion in interest payments each year. How much of our Golden Society can be financed by $400 Billion each year? How much of your money goes to pay bankers $400 Billion annually?

The second part of the Friedman/Money Masters solution is to raise the fractional reserve requirement in direct proportion to the amount of debt based currency replaced until all of the money is replaced and the reserve requirements are at 100%. This step will prevent banks from artificially inflating the money supply by creating additional currency out of thin air through fractional reserve loans. With reserve requirements at 100%, private banks will no longer be able to create money as debt, and the money supply will stabilize.

This is an excellent, workable solution, but there is one part that doesn't sit well with me. Much of the debt is held by the Federal Reserve and other central banks. Their fraud, greed and corruption should not be rewarded by replacing the money/debt that they still hold and which they issued at no cost to themselves. Doing so would put too much financial power back into their untrustworthy hands.

My permutation on the Friedman/Money Masters solution feels more just and fair. Instead of purchasing at full price those bonds still held by the Federal Reserve and other central banks, retire those bonds at pennies on the dollar or simply reclaim the bonds. Put the balance into the General Assistance Fund where it can be spent to help those in need, to eliminate poverty within one generation and to finance the transition to a Golden Society. Justice would be served and that money would go to much better use helping those people who were impoverished by the corrupt, fraudulent system.

The World Bank, the International Monetary Fund (IMF), and the Bank of International Settlements (BIS) are basically international private central banks coordinating the national private central banks. The final part of the Friedman/Money Masters solution is for the U.S. to withdraw from all of these institutions until such time as monetary sovereignty has been restored to the world at large.

Imagine a world with no national debt. Imagine a world in which all of your taxes go to public services and none go to interest payments. Imagine ample money for each person to be economically prosperous and to live in abundance. Such prosperity can be our reality and it will take only one year to manifest!

THERE IS NO GOLD

For those who champion a return to the gold standard, you should be aware of this fact. There is no gold, or at least not enough for a free currency. It is estimated that 80% of the world's gold supply has been cornered and is owned by the various private central banks. Fort Knox is empty, or so it is supposed since the bankers won't even allow the U.S. government to conduct an audit. A return to a gold standard would only return control of the money supply to those same bankers.

49

The finite bases of gold standards and other precious metal currencies present another issue. They don't have the means to expand to match economic growth. The inflexibility of a precious metal currency will ultimately manifest as economic constriction. The finite nature also makes it possible for large financial interests to corner and manipulate the precious metal as has happened in the past and as is currently happening with gold.

HAVE HEART

These solutions are simple and easy to implement, but don't assume the bankers will go quietly. Their control of the money supply gives them enormous global political and financial control. Without a major shift in awareness, they won't give that up willingly. Historically, these are ruthless people who have started wars simply to increase their wealth and control. Expect them to use every means at their disposal to maintain power. Hopefully, they will wake up first.

Stand firmly in your hearts. Their control is an illusion. Human hearts focused on freedom and justice can prevail against any odds. Truth and virtue are on our side.

In a Golden Society, poverty will be eliminated within one generation. Abundant wealth will become the standard. Eventually, money will no longer have meaning and will become obsolete. This makes perfect sense when the maxim, *"As above, so below"* is applied. We live in a universe of infinite energy. As humanity comes to understand this universal truth, we will manifest infinite energy (wealth) on the earth plane. In such a state of unlimited abundance, money will ultimately become an anachronism.

Through *Star Trek*, Gene Roddenberry gifted us with a vision of a moneyless society in which the purpose of life is growth, self-improvement, fulfillment and exploration/expansion. One day, his vision will manifest as reality. Until that day, money should simply be a fair medium of exchange issued by the people's representatives for the benefit of all.

CHAPTER 7
UNIVERSAL EDUCATION

This chapter is quite possibly the most significant in this book. When you understand the premise that life is about growth and learning, and you also understand that education is a means of consciously pursuing those goals, then it easily follows that education is a most vital component of a Golden Society.

For individuals as well as societies, education is the path to freedom, independence and abundance. Education empowers individuals to meet survival and personal needs and to pursue self-realization. It provides the answers to poverty, pollution, crime, discontent, war, disease and every other ill that manifests in modern society. Education frees ingenuity and opens the door to new technologies and methodologies that can transform society and provide each person with ever more harmonious and fulfilling lives. Societally speaking, education provides the best return on any investment of resources.

To understand the possibilities of a system of true education, you must first rid yourself of the current concept. Modern education has two main purposes: to instill unquestioned obedience to authority and to slot its subjects into the great economic machine. Neither of these purposes helps individuals find and attain their True Self nor fits into a Golden Society in any way.

True education develops whole beings. It helps individuals obtain economic and personal independence while providing the means for each person to attain self-actualization. Beings that are physically healthy, emotionally stable, intellectually developed, economically abundant and personally fulfilled are generally productive,

51

beneficial contributing members of society. They do not produce the drag on society that is generated by the negative effects of ignorance and poverty.

The cost of providing education is far lower than the cost of dealing with the consequences of ignorance. Have you ever wondered that a year of Ivy League education costs less than keeping a maximum security prisoner for a year? An Ivy League bachelors degree takes only 4 years, yet a prison sentence can last a lifetime.

There are not many Ivy League graduates who are guilty of drive by shootings or who need welfare assistance. When you consider that the Ivy League is among the most high-priced educations available, it becomes obvious that, in the big picture, education represents an overall savings. It is a short term expense with long term benefits that reduce direct and indirect costs to society.

Reduced costs are the economic benefits. Don't lose sight of the greater benefits of education: higher quality of life and fulfillment for individuals and society as a whole. A proper education system that produces healthy, productive, fulfilled individuals would pay for itself just from the savings garnered in other sectors of society: law enforcement, penal system, wellness care, welfare, food stamps, etc.

There are means of directly funding education, providing maximum benefit to all for relatively small cost. How a society spends its resources is a statement of its priorities. In a Golden Society, the largest portion of the public budget will go to education.

General Education, education common to all citizens, aids them in becoming physically, emotionally, mentally and spiritually healthy, well integrated, highly functional individuals. General Education should be provided directly from public funds. In a Golden Society, General Education would be analogous to current public school education but on a much more encompassing scale.

Initial Career Education, analogous to current university and trade school education, should be provided directly from public funds when possible. As we convert to a Golden Society, it may take a few years for sufficient funds to come available to provide for all

Initial Career Education. In that case, education loans can be made to students from the General Assistance Fund.

The same principle applies here as with wellness care. Funds for education can be lent at no or low interest and the loans can be tracked electronically. Once the student gains employment, a percentage of any income above the poverty line will go to repayment of the loan, replenishing the GAF and providing the means to help others.

Debt is presently used as a means of enslavement. The current student loan system is one of the worst culprits. Student loans are not subject to the Truth in Lending Act, bankruptcy laws or other consumer protections.

Many students leave school saddled with debts that follow them for life. High interest rates and unstable economic conditions mean that often years and even decades after graduation, students' debt burden is higher than that with which they left school. Many students end up as debt slaves working their entire lives in servitude to banks.

By providing the financial means for every citizen to obtain an education, the education ceiling artificially imposed by current financial barriers will be removed. Any person who is motivated to do the work and get the necessary grades can get any education they need to achieve any goal they have. The means of loan repayment will not cripple them financially as they start out in the world.

Ongoing Education is any education that is undertaken after Initial Career Education is completed. Ongoing Education may be, but is not necessarily, related to career education. It could be anything from obtaining a second Ph.D. to learning how to scuba dive to learning how to cook in a new style to learning how to meditate. Any of these fields can be pursued simply for self-enrichment or as a path to another career.

A scuba diver can enjoy diving reefs and wrecks, but may also eventually become a Dive Master or Dive Instructor. The life of a cooking student may be enriched by new styles of food preparation, but he or she may also end up as a professional chef or restaurant owner. A Golden Society recognizes that all education increases quality of life and fulfillment, having a positive effect on the individual involved and society as a whole. Its worth is irrefutable, and the return cannot be measured in dollars alone.

Yet, since Ongoing Education is more about fulfillment and obtaining the higher levels of the hierarchy of needs, General and Initial Career Education have priority of public and General Assistance funds. In a Golden Society, there will, in a matter of a relatively few years, be more than enough funds for all education. Initially, as the transition takes place, citizens will be expected to pay for part or all of their Ongoing Education.

It will take a year to institute monetary reform fully. Two to three years will be needed to make major inroads with free energy. Other reforms may take up to five years to be felt. That much time may be required to reap enough financial benefit to have the necessary money to publicly fund all or even part of Ongoing Education. Until then, part of the cost can be borrowed from the GAF. The remainder will have to be paid for individually. As reforms take effect and the financial strength of the Golden Society grows, public funds can pay increasingly higher percentages of Ongoing Education.

Ongoing Education not only helps create a happy, fulfilled populace, it also helps create a flexible, dynamic work force. Easily obtained Ongoing Education facilitates career changes as society evolves and economic structures shift. Thus, there will be no need to artificially prop up failing industries to maintain an employment base. This will be another savings generated by a Golden Society educational system.

With the introduction of free energy along with monetary, tax and wellness care reforms combining to save money and increase spending power for each individual, there will be ample funds to devote to universal education. The direct and indirect benefits of universal education will collectively save even more, creating a spiral of savings and benefit that outweighs the initial investment.

Some people may be concerned that too much spending on education will hurt the economy. A revolution in thinking is needed to understand the direct economic benefits of a society that prizes education.

Who says that a healthy economy depends on the number of cars produced or the amount of oil pumped? That is a fallacious precept promoted by those who benefit from it. Universal education is actually an important economic driver in a Golden Society. There will be many more teachers gainfully employed. There will also be administrators to run the schools, construction jobs to build them, and maintenance jobs to care for them. All of these professionals will be productive members of society, contributing valuable services, generating and spending income, and paying taxes.

Referring to education in the old paradigm, someone said, "Those who can't do, teach." This statement shows ignorance of and lack of respect for education and educators. Teachers should be some of the more valued and honored members of society. They do no less than lay the foundation for the future. Ultimately, virtually every member of a Golden Society will be a teacher at some point.

The saying really should be, "Those who can, do, and then teach." In a life well lived, an individual learns a skill or a battery of skills. They practice those skills through career or hobby until becoming highly proficient, many even attaining mastery. Then, at some point, they will pass on their skill and wisdom to another generation through teaching, formally or informally.

Whether in rocket science, martial arts, basket weaving or folk music, by seeking fulfillment through self-development, each individual should develop skills worth passing on to others of like interest. Learning and teaching should be done by each of us throughout our lives. They are honored parts of any conscious civilization.

GENERAL EDUCATION - INFANCY

General Education begins at infancy. Actually, it begins *prior to* infancy, in the womb. A well educated mother understands that her physical and emotional states affect her unborn child. By properly physically nourishing herself before and during pregnancy, the gestating child receives the nutrients and energy it needs. It learns on a primal level that it lives in a world of plenty and will have the resources required for a fulfilling life.

Similarly, if prior to and during pregnancy, the mother maintains a peaceful emotional state and lives in a stress free environment, the child learns that it lives in a safe world. It is born with more emotional balance. Hence, it can easily be argued that education begins in the womb and actually begins with the education of the parents.

From the earliest days of infancy, a child's brain needs to be stimulated. The more the brain is stimulated at an early age, the more nervous system connections are developed that serve the being throughout its life. Early nervous system development can be compared to increasing the complexity of computer hardware, allowing more sophisticated software to be run for the life of the computer.

In a Golden Society, General Education provides facilities for parents to bring infants to be stimulated in group settings using music, color and many other means. It also educates parents on methods to create nurturing, stimulating environments at home, so that infants can receive this stimulation throughout the day.

Highly developed brains in emotionally balanced children set the foundation for a productive, well adjusted, fulfilled citizenry. Any cost of this early education is repaid through reduced need for the rehabilitation and maintenance of emotionally maladjusted, unfulfilled, poorly educated citizens.

The dysfunction of current society has created a vast number of emotional issues, along with physical ailments, throughout the population. As we transition to a Golden Society, additional resources will need to be dedicated to address these ills, particularly in children. If we can correct the ills at a young age, we can create a healthy generation that will then create subsequent healthy generations.

Children should be observed for signs of emotional and physical distress. Upon discovering signs of emotional trauma in a child, not only should the child receive the counseling, therapy and support it needs to heal, but the parents should receive the same support so the source of the problem can be healed as well. Then, the child will have a more nurturing, supportive environment in which to grow and reach its potential.

In the case of physical ailments such as obesity, once the problem is diagnosed, an investigation should be made into the source of the situation: is the problem diet? glandular dysfunction? emotional stress? lack of exercise? Parents and child can then be shown solutions and given the additional education and support needed to implement them. The earlier the cause is diagnosed and addressed, the greater the life of happiness, health and functionality the person will attain.

In a Golden Society, General Education begins in the womb and earliest infancy and continues throughout life, seeking to help each individual become physically healthy, emotionally balanced, intellectually stimulated, economically independent and spiritually fulfilled.

GENERAL EDUCATION - EARLY YEARS

"... Muad' Dib learned rapidly because his first training was in how to learn. And the first lesson of all was the basic trust that he could learn. It is shocking to find how many people do not believe they can learn, and how many people believe learning to be difficult."

FROM *DUNE*, BY FRANK HERBERT

Once again, Frank Herbert showed how far ahead of his time he was. I often think one of the greatest gifts my parents gave to me was telling me from an early age that I was smart and could learn anything I wanted and be anything I chose. I wonder how much of being selected for 'gifted' class and other advanced learning had to do with the actual brain power with which I was born and how much of it had to do with my parents making me believe that I had the capacity for those selections.

One of the first lessons children should learn is that they can learn. They should also be taught how to learn. In the current education system, children are put into a classroom, information is thrust at them and they must cope as they can.

An education system whose purpose is the life development of the individual first teaches students how to learn. Everything from how to take and organize notes, to mnemonic devices that improve capacity for memorization, to speed reading, to a plethora of other incredibly useful learning techniques should be taught at the youngest age that they can be assimilated. Students will then have the skills of learning that can be applied to all aspects of life. Back to our computer analogy, if early stimulation increases hardware capacity, learning techniques increase input capacity and reduce download time.

Another primary lesson all children should learn is that learning is a fun, natural part of life and will continue to the end of one's days. Human beings are born learners and explorers. Several years ago, I saw an amazing time lapse film of a mother sitting at a table in a coffee shop talking with friends. She put her infant on the floor. The time lapse photography was able to show the definite pattern of the child's movements. The infant crawled away from its mother, investigated a portion of the room, then crawled back to its base. This pattern repeated itself as the child explored new sections of the room, always with returns to the safety of its mother/base between trips into the unknown, until the child had explored the entire room.

Learning and exploration are hardwired into our beings. At our deepest levels, this is who we are as individuals and as a race. We explore, return to base, then stretch the envelope again. Unfortunately, the current education system dampens this instinct or crushes it out entirely.

I can recall from my public school days that learning was no fun. We were stuffed into classes and information was shoved at us. We were told to learn it and that our futures depended on our ability to conform and to assimilate the information. Many of my friends hated it as much or more than I did. I was sad when I came to understand that they associated that unhappiness with learning in general rather than with the system of rigidity and control. Most were determined to just get through it and, upon graduation, never learn again.

I have seen this attitude time and again in many people I have met throughout my life. So many people have stagnated on emotional and intellectual levels that we now have a society of mental and emotional teenagers walking around in middle aged bodies. For many people, change and growth stop upon graduation from high school. Rather than promoting growth, learning, and evolution, the current education system results in stagnation and atrophy. This may benefit those seeking cogs to insert into the economic mill, but it is anathema to a society whose purpose is the growth and fulfillment of each individual.

The foundation of early General Education, the awareness that everyone can learn, that learning is fun, and that there are techniques to make learning easy, is a cornerstone of a Golden Society. Once invested with these understandings, each individual is empowered to learn throughout life, finding and attaining the fulfillment that is unique to each of us.

GENERAL EDUCATION - INTERMEDIATE YEARS

Once infancy and early education have increased hardware and input capacity, it is time to download software. Rather than being weighted to the intellectual, comprehensive education addresses the entire being: physical, mental, emotional, economic, social and spiritual. We need to look beyond the concept of children sitting in desks staring at information written on blackboards, in books or on electronic pads. That certainly is part of the equation, but there is so much more young minds and bodies need to be stimulated and healthy.

Music has been shown to develop brain connections at an early age. It affects thinking and reasoning throughout life, expanding hardware capacity. Music should be an essential part of learning from the very beginning and throughout General Education. Not only are there educational benefits, but music also provides a lifetime of fulfillment and joy. Imagine a society in which each person can play at least one instrument. The possibilities for personal interaction and creative expression are limitless.

Art develops creativity, right brained thinking, self-confidence and personal expression. It also provides an outlet for emotion and helps create balance in that area. As such, it should be a consistent part of the General Education curriculum from the earliest ages.

Dance is an ancient form of social interaction and personal expression that seems to be programmed into each of us. Dance is a primal part of our beings. Learning dance develops coordination and physical fitness, but just as importantly, it develops social skills and helps overcome shyness and self-consciousness. Dance should be part of the General Education curriculum for each person from the time they are able to walk until they graduate.

Martial arts develop conditioning, coordination, flexibility and self-confidence. They also instill discipline, focus and mental toughness. The practical capability of defending oneself is a benefit throughout life as is the confidence it instills. Martial arts should be a regular part of General Education from the early years onward.

Team sports are fantastic as fun ways to develop teamwork and cooperation along with physical fitness, coordination and conditioning. Yet, as much as I enjoyed them in my childhood years, they are difficult to translate to adult life. As other responsibilities take greater shares of our time, it is very difficult to get a sufficient number of adults together on a regular basis to play team sports enough to maintain proper conditioning and fitness. Hence, yoga, pilates and chi kung along with martial arts, dance and other individual fitness systems should be taught as part of General Education. These skills will serve the students throughout their lives as they will have the means of maintaining their fitness levels on individual bases.

In addition to providing a necessary component of a comprehensive education and providing social stimulation and interaction, these physical activities give young bodies the movement and exercise they need in order to sit through mental exercises more easily and comfortably. Physical training is a necessary component of successful intellectual education.

Mental training has been the cornerstone of the current educational system and will remain a critical component in a Golden Society. Mathematics teaches logic, critical thinking and problem solving. Language develops communications skills as does writing and typing. Sciences develop understanding of the world in which we live. History helps us understand from where we came and, hopefully, helps us avoid repeating mistakes. Assimilating these subjects will be made easier thanks to the learning skills developed in early years.

Meditation develops focus, concentration and self-discipline. It also helps to balance the emotions and reduce stress. These, in turn, increase physical health and well being. Meditation practice should begin in the early years and continue throughout General Education.

Healthy diet and proper nutrition are essential parts of maximizing fulfillment in a balanced life. With organic food, clean water, and pollution free energy, general health will improve accordingly. Educating students about healthy diet and nutrition completes the process.

In the current paradigm, profit takes precedence over health. Education about diet and nutrition is meager and often discouraged. By maintaining such a low level of general nutrition, not only do food conglomerates prosper, so does the medical industry.

Education about diet and nutrition should begin at a young age and continue throughout General Education. Since every person is different and physiology changes over time, children should be regularly tested for food allergies, constitutional intolerances and harmful food combinations. Among the benefits of eliminating these dietary hazards are improved immune system function and mediation of chemically driven behavioral imbalances. Over time, students can come to know the foods that best support their individual physiologies and learn how to prepare those foods.

As the exercise regimen and wellness schooling requirement of General Education take effect in the younger generation, the overall wellness of the population will improve. Over time, generation after generation will pass through this wellness education system. Not only will quality of life increase, but wellness care costs will reduce, offsetting that portion of the cost of education.

As students attain their later years, school kitchens should become class rooms. By preparing food for the younger students, older students can practically apply the knowledge they have gained. Not only is this practical application an excellent teaching tool, it is a cost savings for the education system.

GENERAL EDUCATION - LATER YEARS

In the later years of General Education, obviously many of the subjects previously studied will be continued in greater depth. Other subjects will also be introduced. Civics should be taught so each person has an understanding of the workings of government. Personal economic management will teach how the financial system works and how to budget and make financial plans to achieve life goals.

Basic survival is another skill that should taught in General Education. Not only will survival skills save lives in crisis situations, they also teach self-reliance and instill self-confidence. There should be a grounding in basic first aid for every student and they should also learn basic survival skills in the event they are stranded in desert, mountain, jungle, arctic, woodland and other environments. Advanced classes can be taken voluntarily, but each student/citizen should know how to find or build shelter, signal for help, access clean water, search for food and defend him or herself in a crisis.

The goal of General Education should be to give each citizen the knowledge and skills needed to live happy, healthy, functional, productive lives and to prepare them for their Initial Career Education.

LEARNING CAMPUSES

In a Golden Society, schools will be much more than a building or collection of buildings. They will become beautiful campuses, relaxing, nurturing, safe and stimulating. They will be more than just educational institutions. They will become safe havens, places of recreation and activity, and homes away from home for the children. Instead of dreading going to school, children will look forward to it based on the positive experiences they have there.

The school day and school year will evolve as well. Right now, our school day and year are still based on the needs of an agrarian nation. Originally, students were given the summer off to help on the farm and assist with the harvest. School days were based on the farming day and with the idea that parents would be at home to receive the children once the school day ended.

These parameters have changed drastically in the last century. Most of the population lives in urban and suburban centers. Many families are single parent households. In two parent households, both parents often work full time either out of choice or economic necessity. As such, it is a difficulty for children to be released from school between 2 and 3 p.m. while most parents work until 5 or 6 p.m. or even later.

The school year can be changed to year round (as moans of anguish come from the children!). There can still be vacation time built into the school year, but rather than one huge block during the summer, it can be broken into smaller blocks throughout the year. Families can plan their vacations around these breaks. During breaks in which a family has no vacation plans and the parents must dedicate their time to work, children can still be taken to the learning campuses. There, they can participate in structured, supervised recreational activities with their school mates, as well as receive extra tutoring and instruction as needed.

If a family's travel plans don't coincide with scheduled school breaks, it will be simple to load lesson plans and activities onto hand held pads and to maintain communication with teachers electronically so the students can keep up with their course work while on vacation.

The school day will also evolve to be more family friendly. There will still be set hours in which formal classes will be taught. But, the learning campuses will be accessible for many hours before and after that time. If a parent has an early shift, their children can be dropped off at the learning campus with peace of mind, knowing their children will be safe while participating in supervised recreation and social time, as well as extra study and tutoring as needed.

The same is true at the end of the school day. If a parent's work keeps them from getting to school at the time of dismissal, children can stay longer. They can participate in extracurricular activities such as clubs and sports. Once the formal activities have come to a close, they can remain for safe, supervised recreational, social and study time.

I know quite a few single parent and double working households. It is incredible to me the amount of energy, worry and stress these parents go through trying to find qualified babysitting and child care, not to mention the amount of money spent on that care. They also must cope with the loss of work and income that occurs when a problem arises with a babysitter and a parent must stay home to care for their children.

Centralizing child care on learning campuses solves these problems. By integrating infirmaries into the learning campuses, children with minor illnesses and injuries can be given care without disrupting parents' work schedules.

Too many children are currently left completely alone or under the supervision of unqualified caretakers who have no training. The change in school day and year solves that problem, making parenting a much easier proposition while giving children the safety, stability and support they need and deserve.

GRADING

The grading system will change in a Golden education system as well. There will still be a need for testing, but rather than having those test results slot a student into his or her place in the socioeconomic structure, they will be used to indicate the student's strengths and weaknesses so the weaknesses can be addressed while the strengths are further developed.

By testing, I don't mean nationally standardized testing. I am referring to classroom testing of individual subjects to monitor comprehension and retention of information.

There are many different types of intelligence. Each person excels at some and lacks in others. I had a business partner who could barely spell his own name, but he was a mechanical and spatial genius. He could look at a mechanical situation and arrive at a solution in minutes that would take me hours to work out on paper. Yet, in school, his teachers treated him as a failure because his skills weren't those prized by the system.

One of the most ridiculous institutional structures that I have seen is the means of passing students from one grade to another or failing them and holding them back. In my school, there were certain core subjects including math and English. If you failed one core subject, you failed the entire grade and had to repeat the entire year. Absurd. It didn't matter how good students were at the other subjects. By failing a core subject, they had to repeat them all. Such rigidity taught those children to think of themselves as failures and to hate school.

I also had friends who were intellectually brilliant. They did extremely well at the core subjects, even though they were lacking in others. Because the other subjects were deemed nonessential by the establishment, these students were passed on to the next grade.

There should be certain minimums required to graduate from General Education. Testing should be a means of monitoring progress in each subject. When a student is having difficulty with a subject, tutoring, extra study and support should be provided until the student is able to achieve proper proficiency.

The goal of education is to create well rounded, functional, capable, independent beings. Each skill is needed. Since most students will excel in some areas and struggle in others, there will be no stigma attached to receiving extra support where it is needed. Indeed, there are good lessons to be learned in understanding that we all have weaknesses, and they can be overcome with hard work, perseverance and support.

In the current education system, testing labels some children as successes and others as failures. In a Golden Society, testing will be a means of assisting all to success.

INITIAL CAREER EDUCATION

Initial Career Education is the primary education that relates to career training undertaken by a student after completion of General Education. It can include a bachelors degree, a masters degree or a doctorate if those are necessary to a career choice. It can also be a trade education, art education, or even as specialized as a pilots license.

A significant part of creating a Golden Society is empowering citizens to enter careers that not only provide for them financially, but, even more importantly, fill them with passion and joy, challenge their growth, and provide fulfillment. Imagine a society in which each person is a college graduate, a skilled craftsperson or both. Imagine all people employed in careers they love. Imagine the hope given to underprivileged children who know that no matter their financial circumstances, they can receive any education needed to achieve any career goal and fulfill any dream. Understanding the benefits of a fully employed, financially self-sufficient, and fulfilled population, it should be clear that public funding of Initial Career Education will pay for itself in more than just financial terms.

A population that is gainfully employed in fulfilling careers results in reduced government expenses and a broader tax base. Crime is reduced, health improves, and the need for subsistence benefits is eliminated. Because everyone who so chooses is employed, the entire population contributes to the public funds in the form of a fair tax system and via increases in money supply resulting from economic expansion.

Within a matter of years, Initial Career Education will be fully funded publicly, provided the student meets the standards of continuing education. During the initial transition to a Golden Society, some of the necessary funds may need to be prioritized to other projects (free energy, desalinization, etc). In that case, public funds will pay for education up to a certain benchmark. The remainder can then be paid from personal funds or through loans from the General Assistance Fund.

ONGOING EDUCATION

Ongoing Education may be related to career change, but it also may simply be for the fulfillment, growth and expansion of the individual. While it is recognized that *any* Ongoing Education increases fulfillment, creates greater harmony and raises quality of life, Ongoing Education has a lower priority for public funds than General or Initial Career Education. It would be ideal to have and eventually there will be sufficient public funds to pay for all Ongoing Education. Initially, though, individual citizens will be responsible for themselves, though the GAF can supplement individual financial resources.

Remember, we are creating a society of independent individuals. We recognize the purpose of Life and are creating a society that empowers its individual members toward the goals of growth, learning and expansion through personal fulfillment. Still, the resources of the society must be prioritized according to need.

The idea here is that once citizens have completed their General and Initial Career Education, they will have the means to be financially independent. There may be a small amount of debt accrued to their General Assistance accounts from loans acquired for wellness care insurance and schooling during their Initial Career Education. Other than repayment of that debt, the money earned from their individual careers is at their disposal.

Thanks to the other reforms presented in this book, there will be far more disposable income per person than ever before. Each citizen can choose to save a portion of their income to dedicate to future education. They can also choose to borrow from the GAF to pay for Ongoing Education.

It is expected that most citizens will choose to change careers at least once during the course of their lives. Economic changes and technological innovation may mandate certain career changes. They may also result from choice based on evolving individual growth and fulfillment needs. It stands to reason that at some point a person will have obtained all of the growth possible from a certain career. Then, remaining in that career will induce stagnation and all of the negative effects that entails. In those cases, change will need to be made.

The General Assistance Fund can be prioritized in favor of career change education over other Ongoing Education. Within a few years of the founding of our Golden Society, there will be ample public funds to pay for all Ongoing Education. Until then, we must spend public funds wisely according to the wisdom of our hearts and allow individuals to make up the difference.

Until the time that all citizens have anchored their consciousness firmly in their hearts and make their decisions from there or from a higher place in their beings, it would be wise to have individuals pay a portion of their Ongoing Education. Whether it is 50% or 25% or even just 10%, having to pay a portion from personal funds will discourage abuse of the system and encourage only serious applicants for Ongoing Education.

Education is a foundation of a Golden Society. It empowers individuals to find and live their fulfillment. It provides society as a whole with the knowledge and wisdom needed to prosper. Free energy, clean water, organic food, health and wellness, financial reform and every other advancement find their roots in education. Education is the spark of innovation, the manifestation of solutions. Whether spiritual, emotional, mental or physical, education is the means for assimilation of current knowledge as well as the basis for advancement. In fact, education is the critical component in ending poverty forever, but that is a matter for the next chapter.

CHAPTER 8
ENDING POVERTY FOREVER

This subject is near and dear to my heart. There is no reason for poverty. Let me say that again. ***There is no reason for poverty.*** Poverty today is artificial and intentionally fabricated. It supplies a ready work force of people willing to do the most dangerous and degrading jobs and provides a pool of cannon fodder for military conflict.

As a result of crippling poverty, pregnant mothers are working with toxic chemicals in dangerous, low paying factory jobs. Children are missing school to labor in mines under dreadful working conditions. Fathers are shipped off to wars in countries they know and care nothing about.

Boss Tweed once infamously stated, *"You can always hire half of the poor to kill the other half."* Maintaining a segment of the population in abject poverty furnishes the ruling class with a ready pool of hands willing to do virtually anything in order to meet their most basic survival needs. Welfare, food stamps, Medicaid and other forms of 'social assistance' are simply means of spending the minimum amount necessary to keep the masses from rebelling violently, while maintaining a sufficient level of poverty to meet the purposes of the plutocrats.

Poverty is also a driver of the current economic engine. Poverty results in physical and emotional health issues, crime and violence. Each of these issues has been turned into profitable industries managed by corporate entities that are owned by the ruling class. Not only is there a pool of workers for the manufacturing, service and war industries, there are also corporately owned prisons and security companies. Medical industries benefit financially from the rampant dis-ease and addiction resulting from the poor diet, unhealthy living conditions and hopelessness stemming from poverty.

In *Star Trek*, Gene Roddenberry presented us with an alternate vision. Humanity eliminates poverty, provides education for all and creates a society in which the goals are the fulfillment of the individual and the advancement of all. Sound familiar? It is completely realistic and attainable for us today! Right here! Right now!

It doesn't matter if you agree or disagree with the motivations for and the causes of poverty stated above. You can research them on your own if you choose. What matters is that the solutions presented here WILL work, regardless of the cause of the situation.

Politicians tend to make a big deal of the few people who do manage to climb out of poverty on their own. Their theory is that if some can do it, all can do it. That theory is fallacious. It is akin to saying that because some people have climbed Mt. Everest, all people can. That perspective doesn't take into account people who are wheelchair bound or have asthma or a fear of heights or other limiting factors. To further this analogy, some people in today's society are born at the summit of Mt. Everest and others have to start from the base with no equipment, supplies or training. That doesn't seem just.

Climbing out of poverty under the current system is extremely difficult. Yet, there is no intrinsic reason for this difficulty. It is artificially created to prevent a portion of the population from doing so. A permanent solution can be created by reallocating the same funds that are being used to confine people in their abject state. It is a simple matter of common sense and compassion. There are cost effective ways to manifest permanent change in socioeconomic status.

By creating permanent change, the resources only have to be allocated once. The costs of imprisonment and of the current social assistance programs that only assuage the situation are open ended. In 2010, Medicaid cost over $389 Billion and Welfare spending was over $429 Billion. Yet, they produced no permanent solution. I liken these false solutions to putting a Band-Aid on cancer. It doesn't cure the disease, but it allows us to ignore it and move on until the situation asserts itself fatally. How many Initial Career Educations can be paid for with $800 Billion? The money is there. We just have to allocate it wisely.

To solve poverty, we must understand that though part of it is financial, part is also behavioral. Finances started the cycle of poverty, but behavior continues and compounds it. People learn by observing. I have seen studies that say that children get up to 90% of their learning through observation. The old "Do as I say, not as I do" maxim simply does not work.

Poverty is multigenerational and has become ingrained behavior. Children grow up observing parents, peers and neighbors in a culture of poverty. It becomes the standard by which they learn and exist.

In a family that has produced medical doctors for generations, the example of earning a medical degree is the norm to children growing up in that family. To them, it is nothing more than an achievable challenge. Conversely, in a family that has existed in poverty for generations, to remain in poverty is the example and expectation. There is no stigma attached to doing so.

In poverty, parents are often uneducated, so the children have no inspiration or example to follow. The cost of higher education seems unattainable and hope is soon lost. Violence is common and becomes accepted. Nutrition is not understood. Diet does not support health. The stress of poverty creates emotional complexes and the resources are not available to address them. Emotional complexes are acted out and imprint ensuing generations with complexes of their own. The situation spirals downward and it is amazing that anyone manages to extricate themselves. Those who do are the exception, not the rule.

The measures already presented in this book will relieve much of the financial and environmental pressures that result in poverty. Free energy will reduce the cost of all goods and services and eliminate direct and indirect energy expense. Monetary, tax, budget, and other reforms will reduce financial pressure.

Yet, these are just financial solutions. Easing the financial strain will help, but we know that life is about fulfillment and growth. To achieve true transformation, behavioral changes are needed and the poverty mentality must be eliminated.

Clean food and water will improve health, as will reduced pollutants. Universal wellness care will allow physical, emotional and mental ailments to be addressed. Universal education will provide the resources for upward growth and career attainment. Most importantly, universal education will provide hope.

With these reforms in place, the impoverished will come to understand that the means exist for them to attain a life of fulfillment and abundance. For many, this will be a completely alien concept that will take time and effort to absorb and accept.

For most people living in poverty, the above measures will be sufficient to attain lives of prosperity and fulfillment. For others who need more support, I want to introduce the concept of **Life Development Centers (LDC)**.

It may be best to describe Life Development Centers through example. Let's take a look at a worst case scenario to see how resources can wisely and compassionately, yet cost effectively, help people in the worst of circumstances achieve permanent, positive change.

For our example, we'll look at an unemployed single parent of three who is functionally illiterate and has emotional issues from childhood abuse. Under the current system, this parent would be given subsistence money, food stamps, Medicaid, etc. His or her emotional problems would never be fully addressed because they are not properly covered. Since untreated emotional abuse patterns are usually repeated, the abuse would translate down to the children.

Despite unemployment and low employment prospects, there may be motivation to have more children since benefits often increase based on the number of children in a family. Nutrition would be nonexistent in a diet composed mostly of starch, sugar and fat. Poor eating habits create physiological imbalances in both parent and children, rob them of energy, affect clarity of thought and produce emotional instability. Drug abuse is a real danger since such living conditions are bound to create depression and addictive behavior.

In a Golden Society, when this parent approaches the administration for help, rather than putting a Band Aid on the cancer, the dis-ease itself will be addressed and cured so the patient can lead a healthy life. The need for assistance is a symptom of deeper issues, particularly once Golden reforms that make life and growth easier have been enacted. Rather than just treating the symptoms, Life Development Centers will have the resources to assist in overcoming these deeper issues.

Upon approaching the administration with a request for assistance, the parent in our example will be directed to a Life Development Center and assigned a coordinator. The coordinator will examine the details of the parent's unique situation and help develop an individual plan for change. The parent and children will move into quarters in the Life Development Center. These quarters will be comfortable, but not luxurious. There, the family can live while addressing their life situation.

Simple but nutritious food will be provided. The children will attend school on the premises or at a nearby learning campus. The parent's days will thus be free to address their situation. Thanks to the General Assistance Fund, they will have wellness care insurance. Facilities located within or near the Life Development Center will provide healing for emotional traumas and medical treatment for physical ailments.

Life Development Centers can be associated with farms, manufacturing or other production facilities. Recipients of LDC support can work part time at the farms or facilities in exchange for the support they receive. The food and finished goods can be sold to defray expenses.

Part of the parent's time will be spent at common tasks such as helping with food preparation or grounds maintenance and part will be spent working on the farm or facility. The remainder will be devoted to life improvement. The coordinator will help to create life goals.

In extreme cases such as this, hope may have been lost for so long that the parent doesn't have any long term career or life goals. The starting point may be as simple as being able to provide food and shelter for the family. As the individual grows and evolves, the coordinator will know how to help set and attain higher goals.

Classes will begin by teaching basic literacy. Then, courses can be taken to complete General Education. Once the prerequisites have been achieved, Initial Career Education can begin. Upon graduation, job placement assistance will be provided. Upon gaining employment, the applicant can go about finding a home and building a life.

Parent and children will be properly nourished and will have gained an understanding of supportive diet. The children will have seen the powerful example of a parent successfully working to change their economic status. They will also have seen emotional ills being addressed and observed proactive participation in personal healing. The children will have continued their General Education with the understanding that they can take career education as far as they choose and are willing to work.

In much less than one generation, the entire family will have raised itself out of poverty. With continuing education and the General Assistance Fund empowering the parent in the event that a career change is needed, the family never need fall into poverty again. The children's children will never know poverty and will have the example of their prosperous and happy parents and grandparent to follow. The cycle will be broken forever and a new pattern established.

When you look at the amount of money spent at federal, state and local levels on food, housing, heating, medical and other assistance, you can see that even this worst case scenario doesn't cost any more than the current system. Unlike welfare programs that can continue indefinitely, this scenario is for a finite period of time and will lead to real change and an end to the need for assistance. Not only that, once their prosperity reaches the point that they earn enough to contribute to the tax base, the family will change from consumers of public resources to contributors.

As with everyone else below the poverty line, General Assistance Fund loans will pay for their wellness care insurance, so that will not be an expense of the LDC. Their education will paid for publicly as with all General and Initial Career Education. The only additional expenses incurred through the LDC are temporary food, housing, coordination and administrative expenses.

Part of these costs will be offset by the sharing of common work and by productive work in the factory or farm. The remaining expenses will be paid by loans from the General Assistance Fund. These will be repaid, as with all General Assistance loans, as a percentage of the parent's income after it rises above the poverty line. Thus, repayment will not create hardship for parent or children, but will recompense the help received and make the money available to help others in the future. That can't be said for any current comparable assistance program.

In the end, even if the General Assistance debt is not fully repaid in the recipient's lifetime, the cost of breaking the cycle of poverty for all ensuing generations is well worth the resources incurred and it is far less expensive than a single lifetime of subsidies and open ended social assistance.

I am a big believer in helping others to help themselves. In my experience, Life seems to follow this ethos as well. The above is a functional plan that will help those in poverty to help themselves.

I am certain there will be many permutations off of the main idea as others apply their genius to this solution. The most important factor is that any help given should be to create permanent change in the lives of those in poverty and to bring them to a place of self-sustainability and financial independence. We will all benefit for generations to come. Thus, in our lifetime, poverty CAN be eliminated permanently!

CHAPTER 9
TAX AND BUDGET REFORM

I t will take a revolution in thinking to reach the understanding that taxes can actually benefit a society. We have become so imprinted by the injustice of the current system that jaded skepticism has become the norm. Any and all taxes are looked upon as anathema. It is small wonder. The current system is a means of control. It is immoral, illegal and unconstitutional.

The corrupt tax policy goes hand in hand with the fraudulent monetary system. Income tax was instituted as a means to pay the national debt. It is no coincidence that the Federal Reserve, the IRS in its current form, and the income tax were created at the same time. The Federal Reserve creates the debt. The IRS taxes your labor to pay it.

The Federal Reserve and private banks create money and loan it to the government. The government then taxes the people and uses the revenue to pay interest and principal to the bankers for money that should rightfully belong to the people in the first place. It is a first class scam that has been bleeding the public for a century. In 2010, the interest paid on the national debt was over $375 Billion. How much can society benefit from an extra $375 Billion each year? How many projects can be supported? How many educations can be paid for with those savings?

We have seen that reforming the monetary system will restore the creative power of issuing money to the people. We will now see how, in a Golden Society, taxes can actually benefit the people significantly.

Many people espouse the idea that all government is bad and that government cannot do anything as efficiently as private business. Personally, I feel this perception has been promoted by the banking and corporate interests to garner more power for themselves. The fallacy of this perception lies in the belief that the profit motive is the dominant motivation for human behavior.

This simply is not the case. Even now, in this greed and profit based society, millions of people are willing to work diligently and efficiently at charities and public works for the common good while desiring in return only a humble income to allow them self-sustainability. As the heart chakra consciousness of a Golden Society manifests, ever more people will understand our connected interdependence and will be willing to work for the common good rather than personal profit.

Government is a means of providing common goods for the common good. Its purpose is to provide fairly the goods and services that benefit society as a whole. If the term 'government' leaves you with a bad taste, terms such as 'central' or 'public' or 'common' can be substituted. They amount to the same thing.

Despite propaganda to the contrary, it is possible to staff a government with talented, dedicated people committed to selflessly working for the common good. This is particularly true in a heart-based society. In fact, when a just system is put in place, it will be inundated with volunteers aspiring to do just that.

Government needs resources with which to provide common goods and services. Some of these resources will come from the creation of new money each year as the money supply expands in proportion to economic growth. The remainder must come from taxes. These taxes will be contributions to the common good for the benefit of all.

Once again, the solution is simple. Complexity was built into the current code as a means of control. Far greater benefit can be achieved by implementing a simple, just and effective system.

In a Golden Society, all federal taxes under the current system will be eliminated. This includes income tax, excise tax, corporate tax, inheritance tax and all other current federal taxes. These will be replaced by a single flat sales tax on all goods and services sold for final consumption, excepting purchases for basic needs.

This sales tax will probably begin a little higher as we transition to our new society. As reforms are implemented and the associated savings are realized, the tax rate will decrease accordingly. Eventually, it will settle at or below 10%.

Responsibility for General Education will be transferred to the federal government, included in its budget and paid from this new tax. Doing so will fairly apportion education expenditures nationwide while relieving state and local governments of the tax burden of education. Citizens of individual states and municipalities will be free to vote on additional taxes within their specific areas.

That's all there is to it. It really is that simple!

THE PLAN

Replace all existing federal taxes with a flat sales tax on all goods and services sold for final consumption except certain food, clothing, shelter, wellness care and education.

EXEMPTIONS

The necessities of life: food, clothing, shelter, wellness care and education are the right of every human being and as such should not be taxed. These exemptions should be well defined to prevent abuse of the system.

Food: Organic whole food that provides nutritional benefit is a necessity of life and should not be taxed. Health degrading 'foods' such as refined sugar and saturated fats are discretionary and should indeed be taxed to help pay for the wellness care and other costs they incur. Buying these items is a choice. They are a luxury, not a necessity. The same holds true for alcohol, tobacco, recreational drugs and other items that have negative health effects while providing little or no nutrition.

Clothing: Clothing is a necessity of life. It is on the survival level of the hierarchy of needs. As such, essential clothing should not be taxed. But, ball gowns, tuxedos and other luxury items are a different story. They are nonessential, discretionary and subject to taxation. A ceiling for the cost of essential garments should be set. At current prices, $100 is a fair amount. At a maximum of $100 per garment, a quality, functional wardrobe can be created. Any item over $100 would be considered discretionary and would, therefore, be taxed.

Shelter: Primary housing is another basic necessity of life and as such will be exempt from taxation. This exemption does not apply to vacation homes, second or third homes or investment properties. In the case of rentals, rent for a primary residence will not be taxed, but the purchase of the rental property by the landlord will be.

Wellness Care: Health, by definition, is an essential part of a healthy life. As such, wellness care will be exempt from taxation. Wellness care insurance premiums will be tax free as will the services they provide. Other forms of wellness care that may not be covered by insurance policies but can be purchased by individuals deserve exemption as well.

Massage, Rolfing, reflexology and other modalities that help maintain wellness and prevent disease are of great benefit to quality of life and reduce health care costs as a whole. Someday, all of these modalities will be covered by wellness care insurance. Until then, they will be tax exempt when purchased individually.

Education: We have discussed at length the benefits of education in a society of the heart. Most education will be publicly funded and will be exempt of taxes. Additionally, any portion of continuing or any other education paid for individually will be tax exempt.

ADDITIONS

The tax code should not be used to manipulate behavior. Choice is honored in a heart-based society. Yet, there are certain activities engaged in by some that increase costs for all. In these cases, a means of compensating for those costs is justified. This includes foods, alcohol and drugs that degrade health. Despite the rantings of their lobbies, it is fact that refined sugar, high fructose corn syrup, aspartame, saturated fat and other 'foods' have major adverse health effects. The same is true for alcohol, tobacco and recreational drugs.

A Golden Society does not illegalize these products. That removes individual choice and criminalizes human behavior. Even so, the added societal costs caused by consumption of these products must be taken into account. A health surtax will be added to health degrading products. The additional money collected will be apportioned directly to the insurance mutuals based on the number of members of each mutual. This surtax will directly offset the increased health costs caused by consumption of these products.

Most people will see the wisdom and fairness of this plan and will take the additional expense into account when they choose to purchase these products. As awareness levels increase over time, demand for these products will decrease. Use will decline and abuse will be eliminated.

INDIVIDUAL BENEFITS OF THE GOLDEN TAX CODE

Full Paychecks: The first and most obvious benefit will be no more income tax! When you earn an amount, that is exactly what you will receive. If you earned $1000.00, your check will be for $1000.00 not for six hundred dollars and change after taxes have been extracted. Your money will be yours and you will be able to choose how to spend it.

Choice: Each individual gets to choose if and when they pay taxes. Since the necessities of life are tax exempt, taxes will be discretionary. Buying a luxury yacht or skateboard or smartphone is a choice and will include a tax payment. Anyone who doesn't want to pay the tax can choose not to make the purchase.

An individual can choose to spend money only on necessities and save the remainder. Interest and investment income will be tax free. This will encourage savings, increase the pool of capital and reduce interest rates, stimulating economic growth.

Lower Prices: A sneaky way that politicians indirectly tax the people is through corporate taxes. It is popular with the masses to 'let wealthy corporations pay the taxes.' But, when corporations are taxed, they simply pass the cost to the public through higher prices. The people don't notice the tax when it is integrated into the price of the product, so politicians are able to increase revenue without drawing public ire.

Without being wise to the situation, the people are taxed as surely as if a sales tax proportional to the corporate rate was directly added. With corporate taxes eliminated, prices will fall. Competition will ensure that prices decrease to reflect the corporate savings.

True Inheritance: One of the most insidious and immoral taxes is the inheritance tax. This money was already taxed when it was earned. Then it will be taxed again simply for passing it on to one's heirs.

As I traveled the world, one trait I discovered to be true for all people regardless of culture is the desire of parents to pass on a better life to their children. Inheritance tax directly interferes with this basic human drive.

Under the new tax code, not only can inheritance be passed on free of taxation, money can be exchanged freely as gifts without any tax burden at all. Parents no longer will have to set up trust funds or play other legal games to help their children financially.

Simplification: No more April 15th!!! Well, there will still be an April 15th on the calendar, but it will just be another Spring day. Individuals will never need to fill out another tax return or spend personal resources to pay a tax service to do it for them. This savings of time and money is another increase in quality of life.

As a former businessman, I was extremely frustrated by the amount of time and money spent to figure taxes. Payroll software and annual software updates had to be purchased. A bookkeeper had to be paid to do the data entry. Time had to be spent making monthly and quarterly filings. A CPA had to be paid to do the final audit and annual return. There were fines and penalties when a filing was incorrect or late. A portion of my personal time had to be shifted from productive business operations to attend to tax matters. The result was higher costs and reduced efficiency.

I only ran small businesses. I can imagine the tax accounting costs associated with larger entities. These expenses are built into the cost of the final product and the people again end up bearing the burden. The complexity of the current system creates another hidden tax on the consumer.

In a Golden Society, the simplicity of the tax code eliminates this expense and prices will drop accordingly. Sales tax will be collected as it always has been, a simple matter of a fixed percentage.

With modern technology, it can be simpler still. Bar codes can register an item's tax status. When it is rung up, the tax is added automatically. The tax money can then be electronically diverted to a separate tax account. Just as credit card purchases are batched periodically to a central bank, the sales tax can be automatically batched to the appropriate agency. The entire process can be paper-less. Once the software is installed, the business need spend no time, resources or payroll on tax collection and payment.

COLLECTIVE BENEFITS OF THE GOLDEN TAX CODE

Economic Expansion: We have already discussed many reforms such as free energy and monetary reform that will stimulate the economy. Even disregarding those, the economy will explode simply from the benefits of this tax reform as we convert to a Golden Society.

This tax code is a dream come true for business people and consumers alike. Citizens will have all of their earnings disposable for their use. Savings will be encouraged, creating a larger pool of money at lower interest rates available for loans for capital investment and business expansion. Lower prices encourage increased spending. Foreign investment will increase. Jobs will be created.

Offshore Money: Currently, there are billions of dollars being held in offshore accounts to avoid the tax bite when they are brought home. As soon as this tax code is put into effect, that money will return, infusing the economy. This freed up cash will stimulate the economy to new cycles of growth and hiring.

<u>Foreign Investment</u>: With no matching payroll taxes, no corporate income taxes and no excise taxes, foreign businesses will flock onshore to open factories and research facilities, and to invest in American businesses. Exports will soar. Even with higher wages for American workers, it will be more profitable for foreign businesses to relocate here than to stay in countries with punitive tax codes.

As employment nears 100%, wages will be driven up. As wages rise, discretionary spending will increase. Tax revenues will rise without increasing the tax rate. Everyone benefits, except perhaps tax accountants and the IRS!

FAIR TAX

Kudos to the people who originated and support the Fair Tax plan. I came up with the basics of the plan presented in this book long before I ever heard of the Fair Tax, which was written to provide a sensible alternative to the current tax code.

The Fair Tax is the closest to this plan of any tax reform proposal that I have seen, but it doesn't take into account the broader concepts and other reforms of a Golden Society. Nevertheless, it is a well conceived, creative solution, and I want to acknowledge that.

The greatest credit to its potential viability and efficacy is the vast amount of resistance it has received from the establishment. Kudos for a job well done. I honor anyone with the courage and willingness to think outside the box.

BUDGET

There are two main revenue sources for the government: taxes and newly created money. Now that we have addressed both sources of the revenue stream, it is time to discuss spending.

The current budgeting process is dysfunctional. No account is taken of how much money is available. Politicians decide how much they want to spend, more often based on campaign promises and political favoritism than on fiscal responsibility. They then borrow the money needed to make up the difference between revenue and expenditures. This system suits the bankers, who get to create the money and loan it at interest to the government. But, it is not sound financial practice. Any business or individual conducting its affairs this way would soon find itself bankrupt.

Fortunately, this solution is simple as well. A better system is a Percentage Based Budget. In other words, we decide, based on priorities, the percentage of revenues to allocate to each governmental department. That money is then allocated and those responsible for the departments must create budgets and function using the amount of money available.

For example, if tax revenues for a particular year are $2 Trillion and a certain department gets 10%, then that department will have $200 Billion to spend. The department staff must make a plan prioritizing its spending requirements to meet its goals using the $200 Billion available. This is a real world solution and far more functional than the 'borrow the money we don't have and worry about repayment later' policy that is in place today.

The people's representatives will be responsible for setting the budget percentages. Each year, the legislature will vote on the budget for the upcoming year. Once initial percentages are set, it should take a quorum to change the budget so that it is difficult to alter for political expediency. The following are some of my thoughts on the budget process:

Education: The value of education cannot be stressed strongly enough. It is the best investment of public resources. Period. As such, it should be the most heavily weighted component of the budget, as much as one-third or more. Money for General Education, Initial Career Education and Ongoing Education should be allocated by percentage of the overall education budget.

General Assistance Fund: Initially, this will be a large component of the budget. It will be responsible for assisting the rise from poverty, providing wellness insurance until it can be afforded by all, and funding education loans. The GAF will probably begin at around a quarter to a third of the budget. As the population rises out of poverty and as prosperity and self-sustainability increase, the need for this fund will decrease. It can then be reduced as a percentage of the budget until all remaining need disappears and the fund is no longer required.

Defense: We are not in nearly as much danger as politicians and the ruling class want us to believe. Threats are regularly magnified to create fear as a means of control. Even now, defense spending can be cut drastically without reducing security. As we transition into a Golden Society, danger of international violence will be further reduced. Accordingly, defense spending can be further reduced as potential threats wane.

Infrastructure: As national resources are wasted on foreign wars and bank bailouts, our physical infrastructure is rapidly eroding due to lack of proper maintenance. A solid infrastructure is necessary for a thriving economy and a functional society. Maintaining and improving the infrastructure will create jobs, stimulating the economy directly and indirectly.

As technology evolves, infrastructure needs will change. With the transition to free energy, the electric grid will no longer need to be maintained. Instead, desalinization plants and pumping stations will be built and operated. As anti-gravity technology replaces current propulsion systems, roads and bridges will have less importance.

Having a vital, functional infrastructure for a society is like having a clean canvas for the artist to work. Business and personal creativity can be expressed far more easily. Money devoted to development and maintenance of infrastructure is a sound investment and allows society to function with efficiency and ease.

Research and Development: Business investment in research and development is generally limited to projects that can be translated into profit for the business. After all, the purpose of business is to make profit.

Yet, there is intrinsic value in pure science, advancing knowledge for its own sake. Countless benefits can come out of such exploration. A percentage of the budget devoted to scientific research would be well worth the investment. As we come to better understand the universe in which we live, we can embed ourselves more harmoniously into Life.

Often during pure research, inventions and innovations are discovered that have market value. The rights to these inventions and innovations can be sold to reimburse the expenses that led to their discovery. Thus, the coffers can be replenished from within as well as through tax revenue.

Emergency Fund: Every year, natural and man made disasters occur. Wildfires, floods, tornados, hurricanes and other disasters are inevitable. They are part of life on Earth. Still, it seems as though we are repeatedly caught with our collective pants down. Virtually every time there is a disaster, there are news stories about the financial cost of the disaster and about how the government had to divert resources, raise taxes or borrow money.

A conscious society recognizes that disasters will occur and prepares in advance. Just one half of one percent of a $2 Trillion budget is $10 Billion. That is more than enough money to prepare for and relieve most natural disasters.

With free energy replacing the grid and other technologies coming online, some dangers of disaster can be more easily mitigated. With a proper budget, we can preposition supplies in strategic areas around the country and on board ships to prepare for disasters before they occur and respond to them quickly and efficiently when they do.

MONEY SUPPLY AND THE BUDGET

Public ownership of the money supply and the power to issue money are potent creative tools of the people. As the economy grows, the money supply must increase to maintain price levels and spending power. If a $14 Trillion economy increases by 3%, then it stands to reason that the money supply must increase by 3% as well. Thus, there will be $420 Billion in newly created money. This money can be spent into the economy on a prorated basis according to budget percentages, added to the General Assistance Fund, or loaned to banks, businesses and individuals at prime rates.

WE CAN BOLDLY GO.....

As the economy grows and as poverty related social assistance expenditures decline, the need for taxes will diminish. Eventually the tax rate will be a fraction of what was needed to enact this plan.

In a Golden Society, each citizen will lead a life of prosperity. Every person can live in the comfort and bounty of a modern day millionaire. Most importantly, each will have the abundance to find and live their fulfillment. The Golden Tax Code will create the financial environment to manifest this vision.

One day, money will lose its value and become obsolete. We will transition organically and naturally into a moneyless society such as Gene Roddenberry envisioned.

CHAPTER 10
THE GOLDEN ECONOMY

I often hesitate to use the word 'economy' due to its negative connotations. Some of my earliest memories are of listening in on the news broadcasts that my parents watched. Every night there was a report on Gross Domestic Product and the Dow Jones Industrial Average. I soon came to the understanding that the well being of our society was equated with economic strength and growth. Economic indicators were being used as measures of overall well being. Even as a child, I understood the fallacy of this premise.

As I observed the world around me, I saw people who had plenty of money yet led extremely unhappy lives. I also saw people who were miserable in their pursuit of economic success. I observed an inordinate amount of poverty in a society whose supposed purpose is economic strength and growth. Even more strange, many people who lacked financial wealth led happier lives than many who had greater means. The incongruities struck me.

I also observed pollution, lost habitat, disappearing species, malnutrition, starvation, insufficient medical care, homelessness. These conditions existed because addressing them would not add to the economy. It made no sense to me. When the price is widespread misery, pain and environmental destruction, what is the point of higher economic indicators? Thus, the term 'economy' began to take on a negative connotation in my mind.

I wondered why we didn't have a Quality of Life Index or a Fulfillment Quotient. Those seem to be better indicators of the well being of a society. Health, happiness, fulfillment and free time should be the factors used to determine these.

You should understand very clearly that I have nothing against money or material possessions. That is not my point. But, money is not an end unto itself. Money is a tool, a medium of exchange and a means to help achieve the more important goals of life.

I know for certain that we live in a universe of immeasurable energy and that abundance is our natural condition. Abundance is equally available to all and need not be sought by some to the detriment of others. How many need to go hungry and without shelter so others can have billions? The answer is zero. This is a win-win world.

There is plenty for everyone. The ideas that there is not enough to go around and that some people must go without so others can prosper are complete fabrications. Those concepts are another means of control. So are the economic indicators. Their importance is inflated and used as propaganda to manipulate the populace.

If economic prosperity was the primary factor leading to fulfillment, the ruling class would have been satisfied with their wealth long ago. After all, how many billions does one need to be fulfilled? Instead, they unceasingly quest for more, willing to stand on the misery of others to accomplish their goals. Their very lives are the proof that their propaganda is a lie.

To understand the meaning of 'economy' as I use it, a few axioms must first be understood:

- The purpose of life is learning and growth, leading to fulfillment and expanded awareness.

- The purpose of society is to provide a collective infrastructure for the individual members to achieve their individual life purposes.

- No one member of society is more important than any other. All are deserving of the same opportunities for learning, growth and fulfillment.

- All are connected. What happens to one affects the whole.

- Prosperity and abundance are the natural state. Lack is an indicator that something is amiss.

• Material wealth may enhance, facilitate and empower learning, growth and fulfillment, but is not equated to them and does not supersede them.

An economy can be defined as (1) a means of efficiently exchanging goods and services in pursuit of individual and societal goals, (2) the goods and services of a society taken together as a whole. An economy should be the servant of the people, not the other way around. In a Golden Society, the economy is the means of exchanging goods and services as the citizens pursue their fulfillment through growth and learning.

The success of a Golden Economy is measured by the number of jobs and careers that are fulfilling to the members of society and the level of quality of life of its citizens. Our economy will be completely successful when each person has the means to pursue actively and effectively their fulfillment and self-actualization.

I have seen brilliant work by futurists who have designed cities in which virtually all of the work is automated. There is plenty of food, shelter and medicine for all and there is no need for many of the tedious jobs that have been necessary throughout history. In these examples, I have tried to discover what the futurists think the people of the future will do with their time once the menial work is no longer necessary. In most cases, they do not have an answer. Many futurists come from a primarily mental perspective, exploring the possibilities of technology without integrating that into a broader understanding of human nature.

I have great respect for the work these futurists have done. A Golden Society will incorporate many of the concepts they have pioneered. Through my exploration of human nature and the nature of Life, I am able to fill in some of the blanks to show what life will be like in a society of the heart. The careers, jobs, activities and personal pursuits in a Golden Society are what I call the Golden Economy.

Creative expression is the essence of human fulfillment. As I have observed humanity, I have discovered that there is nothing that brings such joy, fulfillment and growth as the application of human ingenuity and energy to create or discover something new. This can

91

be as grand as the creation of a megalithic sculpture, as humble as a plumber installing pipes in a new house, or as sublime as the exploration of space. Humans are creators and explorers.

As a young man, I realized that the highest expressions of a culture are its artists and its warriors. I still know this to be true. (By warriors, I don't mean 17 year old conscripts sent to war on behalf of plutocratic interests. We'll explore the concept of warriors in greater depth in a later chapter.)

By art, I am not referring to technical proficiency of artistic skill. I am referring to Art in the esoteric sense. Art is the act of creating something never before seen or known. It is a merging of the spiritual and the material expressed through the heart, inspiration manifested physically through technical means.

As a teenager, I was graced with the opportunity to visit the Louvre in Paris. On my way in, I came upon an artist using chalk to reproduce the Mona Lisa on a square of sidewalk. To my untrained eye, it was an amazing replica of the masterpiece. Yet, while it was a work of incredible technical proficiency, it was not Art.

Da Vinci's original is a work of Art. Through painting, he manifested his inspiration to show a woman in a pose never before used, with an expression never previously shown, using techniques and other elements never used before. The street artist, while demonstrating outstanding technical proficiency, was not expressing inspiration. This is the difference between what I refer to as art vs artistic skill.

As humans grow and evolve, each will ultimately gravitate to some form of creative expression based on his or her individuality. Whether it is a new form of wellness care, a new form of propulsion or a new technique for weaving tapestries, in a Golden Society each person will ultimately be an artist in the deeper sense of the word.

That being said, the Golden Economy will integrate harmoniously into the nature of Life and the universe, facilitating full expression of human art and the pursuit of individual fulfillment.

THE INFRASTRUCTURE ECONOMY

A human society needs an infrastructure just as a human body needs a skeleton. A framework is needed to allow the body to function. People will be needed to build, install and maintain free energy devices. Desalinization plants will need to be built, operated and maintained as will fresh water pumping stations. Roads, bridges, seaports, airports, dikes, levees and seawalls must be built, upgraded and maintained. With proper resources allocated, there will be many well paying careers for architects, engineers and craftspeople dedicated to the infrastructure sector.

Living Machines: Sewage and waste disposal is a significant portion of the infrastructure sector that deserves special mention. Throughout human history, the most popular means of dealing with human waste has been to dump it into waterways. As populations grew, sewage treatment was developed, but this mostly entails treating human waste with chemicals and then dumping it into the waterways. In recent decades, creative minds have developed a far more harmonious solution often referred to as Living Machines.

Living machines mimic nature, using natural processes to treat sewage, turning it into clean water and usable products. The raw sewage passes through a series of receptacles containing various living organisms from water hyacinth to snails to beneficial bacteria. These organisms break the sewage down in stages as it passes from container to container. Ultimately, the end product is pure water, as clean as that found in natural streams. In one example of this technology, Japanese koi are farmed in the final tank of a living machine. Since koi are extremely sensitive to environmental toxins, they are living proof of the efficacy of this technology. They also demonstrate how marketable products can be produced from the treatment of sewage.

This technology exists today. It has been in use for several decades on corporate campuses, private estates and municipalities around the world. To use it universally, we only need the collective will to dedicate the needed resources. Imagine if all sewage is converted to clean, potable water without using toxic chemicals. Through living machines and desalinization, there will never again be a lack of fresh water.

Recycling: Recycling will be another major part of the infrastructure economy. As we observe nature, we see that everything is used and recycled. A heart-based, conscious society will seek to mimic this process. As new products are introduced, each will have a plan for recycling or reusing every component. Many components currently made from plastic or other synthetics will be replaced by biodegradable, carbon based components. The technology already exists to replace many plastics with corn starch and other plant based materials. Ceramics will replace others.

The recycling sector will create well paying, fulfilling jobs while reducing the need for raw materials and helping to eliminate the release of toxins into the environment.

THE EDUCATION ECONOMY

Education is a different type of infrastructure, an infrastructure for the body, mind, emotions and spirit. Through it, the creativity of society can be unleashed. As I have said so often, education is one of the most vital, empowering factors in a Golden Society. Its importance cannot be stressed strongly enough.

Education will grow to become a vital part of the Golden Economy. From General Education, to Initial Career Education to Ongoing Education, educators will be needed. The number of teachers will increase dramatically, creating hundreds of thousands of high paying, fulfilling careers.

There will also be careers for education administrators to organize this massive undertaking as well as careers dedicated to building and maintaining the vast network of education facilities. These people will spend their salaries into the economy, stimulating growth and circulating prosperity among all. Currently, the medical industry comprises one-seventh of the U.S. economy. I can easily see the education sector of a Golden Economy growing to a comparable or greater level.

Most members of society will take a turn in the teaching sector at some point in their lives. As each person evolves, there will come a time when there will be great benefit in passing on their learning to others. In the economy today, over 80% of the people work in the restaurant or food service industry in some capacity at some point in their lives. In a Golden Society, I can see the same ratio holding true for the Education Economy.

THE ENVIRONMENTAL ECONOMY

Environmental reclamation and husbandry will be a major part of the Golden Economy. Most of humanity now understands that the environment is a living system in which we exist. For humanity to prosper, the environment must be healthy. It strikes me as odd that while some people can easily see the benefit in maintaining their vehicle and their home, they balk at the idea of maintaining the natural environment. Apparently, they do not see the Earth as their larger vehicle and home.

For a generation or so, there will be a surge in challenging, fulfilling, and satisfying careers in habitat reclamation, toxic waste mitigation and restoration of ecological balance. Once environmental rehabilitation has been achieved, there will be careers for permanent environmental stewards whose jobs will be to monitor and maintain the balance in the ecosystem. There will also be careers for environmental researchers to study nature in all its infinite variety. From what I have observed of human nature, these will be some of the most popular and fulfilling careers in the Golden Economy. The love of nature seems to be ingrained in human genetics.

THE AGRICULTURAL ECONOMY

The human love of nature will be expressed in the agricultural sector as well as the environmental. Many people find great satisfaction digging in the earth and working with animals. Causing things to grow, nurturing life and sharing the bounty fills a deep seated human need.

Even now, there is a movement of educated, prosperous professionals leaving their careers and moving from the cities to return to their roots in the country. There are any number of organic farms, ranches and dairies springing up. Artisan breads and cheeses, organic fruits and vegetables, free range meats and dairy products are becoming increasingly available every day.

These small farms, lovingly tended, fill a much greater need, create far more fulfillment and provide a higher quality of life than employment in mass production, chemically based agribusiness conglomerates. Organic, sustainable private farms also produce higher quality of food and lower incidences of contamination.

With ample clean water, with energy costs eliminated and without the expense of chemical fertilizers, pesticides and herbicides, production costs will drop dramatically. The food supply will become healthier, more nutritious and more delicious even as prices fall.

In a Golden Society, small privately owned farms focused on sound, sustainable and humane practices will provide a safe, healthy food supply while creating satisfying, well paying careers to owners and employees alike.

THE WELLNESS ECONOMY

Health care constitutes one-seventh of the current economy. In the future, health care will be replaced by wellness care. It may account for a similar portion of the economy, but the results will be better. Wellness care seeks to optimize well being and prevent disease. Not only will traditional medical practitioners be part of the Wellness Economy, but so will many other types of wellness professionals. Dietitians, naturopaths, acupuncturists, massage therapists, cranial sacral practitioners, Rolfers, chiropractors and a host of other wellness practitioners will be honored and appreciated members of the wellness industry and the Golden Economy.

In observing humanity, I have seen that the joy of helping others to heal seems to be another ingrained trait. I know many people who derive great satisfaction from their wellness practices. Some of these people had the opportunity to become medical doctors or other higher paying members of the medical industry, but chose their individual practices due to the fulfillment they derive from them.

Not only will the wellness sector create a happier, healthier, better integrated population, it will contribute to the thriving economy by providing innumerable fulfilling, satisfying careers. In a heart-based society, people will flock to work in careers in which they can use their talents to promote the healing and well being of others. The satisfaction of their work will outweigh the desire for extreme compensation. In my experience, these people would be satisfied with a comfortable living wage and the opportunity to be of service to their fellow beings.

THE EXPLORATION AND RESEARCH ECONOMY

Humans are born explorers. From the moment we can crawl, the instinct to explore drives us from within. Collectively, we have that drive as well. While some people are content to tend the home fires, others feel the need to expand the boundaries of our knowledge, to push the envelope of our existence.

In an earlier chapter, the need for pure research was presented. That pure research is the exploration of the nature of the world around us. As our understanding grows, our ability to embed harmoniously into our surroundings increases. We will push the boundaries of space and undersea exploration. As we harness the potential of free energy, new propulsion systems will be developed. In less time than some imagine, the exploration of deep space will be underway.

An entire economic sector will develop to support research and exploration. Some of the best paying and most fulfilling careers will be in this sector. The knowledge developed by our researchers and brought home by our explorers will enhance the lives of each member of society and each succeeding generation. Who knows what discovery or innovation will inspire the next great cultural transformation.

THE ARTISAN ECONOMY

As technology replaces many of the more repetitive and menial jobs, people will have much more time on their hands. This time will be used in the pursuit of creative expression.

Crafts and artisan trades have declined, not due to lack of interest, but because of economic necessities imposed by the current system. If you ask your friends and coworkers what they wish they could do for a living, a significant number of answers will be art and artisan related. Many want to be painters, sculptors, potters, weavers, metalworkers, bakers, woodworkers, leather workers, glass blowers, musicians and other types of artisans and artists. Many fear they can't make enough money in these pursuits, so they hold back.

Humans find great satisfaction and peace in creating with their hands. There is great demand for hand crafted products. This demand will increase as the economy strengthens, prosperity spreads and more people attain the abundance to afford hand made goods. These factors will synthesize in a Golden Society, creating many fulfilling careers in the art and artisan sector.

In the future, homes will be blends of the technologically advanced and the hand made. There will be modern kitchen appliances for preparing food that will be served on hand made pottery, eaten at a custom crafted table under hand blown glass lights. People will come to treasure the unique and the individual. Common items will still be mass produced, but many will be replaced by beautiful and functional works of art lovingly crafted by hand.

With the advent of free energy and a greater portion of the population devoting themselves to artisan trades, hand made items will become ubiquitous and will be affordable for the general population. A significant portion of the Golden Economy will come from this sector as people earn comfortable livings working at trades that serve their passion, bring learning and growth, and fill them with joy and happiness.

THE CONSTRUCTION ECONOMY

The current economy is disproportionally dependent on construction. New home manufacturing is one of the major criteria used today to measure economic health. Even as a child, this never made much sense to me. There are only so many people in the world and only so much land. Why do we have to continue to build new houses? Does economic well being have to depend on infinite expansion of the housing market? What happens to the economy once everyone has a home? Can that energy and those resources be devoted to other purposes?

These questions followed me through my childhood. The answer I found is that construction is an easy way to stimulate job creation. If an artificial need for bigger and better homes can be stimulated and interest rates lowered enough, people will build new homes. The appearance of a healthy economy is created while natural resources are wasted along with the creative genius and energy of those working in that field.

I worked for many years in the construction industry. I found that there are two main types of people doing the work. There are true craftspeople who find great satisfaction in working with their hands and have a passion for the act of creation as they participate in raising a new structure or remodeling an old one. The rest are generally people who are working in construction because those are the only jobs that are available. Many of these people are addicted to alcohol and other drugs to numb the dissatisfaction they feel in living unfulfilled lives without much prospect of advancement.

Construction will remain a major part of a future economy, though methods and practices will change. We will still need homes, schools, public buildings, factories and other edifices. Without artificial stimulation of this sector, there will only be construction of buildings that are actually needed. True craftspeople who find their joy in building will be respected and well compensated members of our society.

It will be fun to watch the construction industry evolve as new technologies blend with old. Adobe and cob construction are ancient building techniques. Mixing clay, sand, water and fiber to create building materials has been done for millennia. The oldest standing and continuously occupied structures on Earth are cob and adobe. These are natural, non-toxic, renewable and extremely inexpensive resources. Clay, sand, straw and other plant fibers are practically omnipresent and are, well, dirt cheap if you will pardon the pun. Adobe and cob are as recycleable as any medium available. When you are finished with them, simply wet, reshape, and reuse them. In addition, cob construction is extremely stable and earthquake resistant.

The main drawback with adobe and cob construction is that they are labor intensive. It takes a great deal of effort to mix clay with water and straw. Then, it must be shaped and either dried in the sun or a kiln. There are automated means of doing this, but they are energy intensive.

With free energy, adobe can be made for literally pennies per block. Without the energy cost, materials for an entire home can be produced for a few hundred dollars.

I really enjoyed seeing the adobe buildings in the *Star Wars* saga. There were also beautiful stone structures. George Lucas showed that even in an advanced space faring civilization, adobe and other natural building materials have a place.

In a Golden Society, there will also be modern structures built with modern materials utilizing advanced technologies. But, there will always be a place for natural building materials. No matter our technological advancement, there will always be homes made from natural materials, furnished and decorated with hand crafted pieces.

Construction will remain a significant part of our economy. It will provide satisfying careers and comfortable incomes for craftspeople while supplying society with safe, efficient, attractive buildings for living, working and playing.

THE MANUFACTURING ECONOMY

Manufacturing will remain a necessity as long as humans live in a three dimensional reality. But, it will evolve to suit the needs of the people rather than use the people to suit the needs of industry. In a Golden Society, manufacturing will be based more on the heart. Profit at any cost will no longer be the motivation.

It was in marketing class that I first heard the term 'planned obsolescence.' I was appalled at the idea that products were deliberately designed to break so they would have to be replaced. The intentional waste of resources and the bleeding of the people's wealth for the purpose of short term profit demonstrated how low the principles of humanity had fallen.

We are indoctrinated with the idea that the free market guarantees the best product at the best price. Planned obsolescence is proof that idea is false. Industry leaders intentionally make inferior products. They have made a science of designed failure. The goal is to have the product fail and be replaced in the minimum time possible without eroding consumer confidence in the product. This is not a conspiracy theory. It is right there in text books and in industry and government publications.

Ecosystems are laid bare, natural resources plundered. Water and air are polluted by toxic manufacturing waste. Landfills overflow. Entire villages are displaced. Human health and survival are put at risk for short term profit. Humanity is not served by the modern manufacturing economy. Only a few individuals that sit at the top benefit while everyone else pays the price.

That will change in the Golden Economy. Durable goods will actually be durable. There is no reason why a vehicle can't last a lifetime, particularly using free energy technology. The same is true for toasters, cameras and washing machines. Affordable replacement parts can be made to extend life even more.

One of the more ridiculous elements of our current economic system is that it is often cheaper to discard a product and buy a replacement than it is to repair it. My printer recently broke. The part that failed was a plastic piece about the size of a quarter, obviously designed to fail. The cost of repair would have been $50-$100 more than replacement of the entire printer. So, the old printer with all of its plastic, glass, metal and associated chemicals went to a landfill. More natural resources were extracted and more toxins released into the environment for want of a component the size of a quarter. Certainly, each of you have similar stories.

Virtually every product we use, when made properly, can last for more than a lifetime. Items will become heirlooms again. Products that truly are made obsolete will have to be replaced eventually.

With proper design, all future products will have a reuse or recycling plan. Manufactured items will also be built on component based systems. If a part fails or becomes obsolete, only that particular component will need to be replaced while the remainder remains in use.

One of the more obvious examples is a computer. In a component based system, when a chip becomes obsolete, it can be replaced with a more advanced chip, extending the life of the computer. When a hard drive fails, only that component will need to be replaced. Today, in most cases, the only option is to buy a new computer.

Materials technology can evolve to become more Earth and human friendly. There are many instances where synthetic materials can be replaced with plant based. Plant starch and fibers provide a non-toxic and renewable alternative to many plastics and other materials. Aluminum and other easily recyclable metals can be used more. Another boon of free energy will be the obsolescence of power lines. There are millions of tons of copper used in the power grid that spans the globe. Copper is a malleable metal that can be useful in many ways. It recycles easily, taking 97% less energy to recycle than to mine.

Ceramics technology is burgeoning. Hi-tech, strong, tough, lightweight materials are being made from clay. With free energy making the firing of kilns an affordable process, ceramics will become a popular material of the future.

Manufacturing will remain an economic sector in a Golden Society and it will remain a profitable industry. Genius will be applied and resources dedicated to make manufacturing serve all of humanity by providing functional, durable, high quality, non-toxic, recyclable products made by people with well paying, safe jobs in healthy, enjoyable environments.

THE ENTERTAINMENT ECONOMY

The final component of the Golden Economy that we will discuss is probably the most fun. The entertainment industry is a vital part of the current economy and will be more so in a Golden Society. When I watch the credits of a blockbuster movie, I am amazed at how many people contributed to its production. Each of those people have well paying, satisfying jobs and the film makes money, often a great deal of money. The same thoughts occur when I visit an amusement park. Many people are employed and the business is profitable. (I just wish they had healthier food!)

We often overlook the entertainment industry when discussing economics, but it is a lucrative sector and it has the potential to be more so in the future. Through the reforms of a Golden Society, there will be far more disposable income. People will spend increasing amounts on entertainment.

We don't often think of them as such, but theater, movies and television are all businesses and are generally profitable ones. The music industry earns billions each year. Millions of people are employed in the entertainment industry and the jobs are often very fulfilling and high paying, particularly for the artists.

Eventually, advertising based income will be replaced by direct payment for entertainment. Commercials are used to create artificial product need to drive sales. Soon, commercials will become obsolete. If people don't know that they need a product, then they probably don't need it. When products are needed, research tools can be used to find the best options.

In a Golden Society, advertising will become extinct. Netflix type entertainment will become the norm. For a fee, a person will be able to choose entertainment options as well as the times and places to enjoy them.

Amusement parks will abound. I still chuckle at George Carlin in *Bill and Ted's Excellent Adventure* when he said that future Earth has more excellent water slides than any other planet we communicate with. In a Golden Society, that will be true! Many places will be built simply for the enjoyment of others. They will generate income and employment as well.

Professional sports is another entertainment industry. Billions are spent each year on television contracts, tickets, merchandise and concessions. (Again, I wish the food was healthier.) As far as high paying jobs are concerned, players, coaches and executives make millions, which are spent into the economy. In a Golden Society, with people leading fulfilling, enriching lives, spectator sports may take on less importance, but people will still pay for the enjoyment and entertainment.

Travel seems to be a common joy for most people. Travel is part of the innate human desire to explore. Just go to any dating website and read the profiles. Almost all profess a desire to travel. I've never read a profile that says, 'I just love my home town and never want to leave.'

Travel is one of the faster growing industries in the world today. It accounts for billions in spending. Some people want to see natural wonders and foreign cultures. Some just want to rest on a beach. Some want adventure. In a Golden Society, a great deal of leisure time will be spent in travel of some sort. Careers in that industry will provide satisfaction, fulfillment and comfortable incomes.

UNSKILLED LABOR

As you read about the economy of the future, it is natural to wonder about menial jobs. Yes, automation will replace many repetitive tasks, but some cannot be replaced. So, who in this scenario will wind up doing the menial tasks? For the most part, they will be done by students.

First, we should understand that any job that must be done in order for society to function effectively is, by definition, a necessary job and therefore important and worthy of compensation. Second, as higher education becomes universally available and more people rise up to find fulfilling careers, the unskilled labor pool will shrink. As with any supply and demand curve, when the labor supply shrinks, wages will rise.

Many students, particularly those undergoing Initial Career Education, will be in need of work. Even if public funds help with tuition and the General Assistance Fund helps with the other costs, students will still need to pay for housing, food, transportation and other life expenses. They can work for a time to save the necessary money, or they can work part time while they are attending school, or they can do both.

Additionally, I know people who prefer labor jobs on a permanent basis. There are people who would love to drive a truck or work a factory job that pays a comfortable wage. They can then use their free time to travel or pursue hobbies and recreation. Artists and inventors can benefit from this as well. A job that pays a living wage without being the primary focus of their life would provide an artist or inventor the finances necessary to support themselves while working on an art project or experimenting on the next great innovation.

Unskilled jobs will become another means of empowerment. They will provide workers with income to pursue their interests while accomplishing tasks needed for the functioning of society.

A REAL LIVING WAGE

Each person that works deserves to make a living wage, meaning enough money to meet the necessities of life including food, clothing, shelter, wellness care, education and the resources needed to pursue personal growth and fulfillment. In the Golden Economy, this will take less money than might be expected.

By removing energy costs that account for 50-90% of the cost of most goods including food, spending power will dramatically increase. Reforming the tax system will cause prices to drop by eliminating the 35% corporate tax rate. It will also result in more disposable income by terminating income tax. Monetary reform will stop inflation from eroding spending power.

These reforms will increase spending power many fold. If we use a low estimate of 2.5 times the current spending power, then, in a Golden Society, a $20,000 annual income will provide the equivalent spending power of $50,000 in today's dollars. That is more than enough money to bring financial independence and create a quality life.

Drawing the poverty line at $20,000 is a very obtainable goal for every person in a Golden Society, thus ending poverty in our lifetime. Just imagine our world today if everyone made at least $50,000 per year. This is easily within our reach.

However, I am not satisfied with $20,000 per person. I want everyone to experience overflowing abundance. A more admirable goal is for each person to earn at least $20 per hour. At 40 hours per week, that comes to over $40,000 per year. With the 2.5 times increase in spending power, that is equivalent to over $100,000 per year in today's dollars. People who earn over $100,000 per year are considered millionaires by some standards, because they have the means to acquire over $1 Million in assets over a lifetime.

At a minimum of $40,000 per year per citizen, we will have created the equivalent of a society of millionaires. Every person will live in ample abundance. Nutrition, wellness care, education, entertainment and personal fulfillment will be within the reach of every person.

Just imagine a society in which the least a person makes is the equivalent of $100,000 per year. Making a minimum of $20 per hour in a Golden Society, some people will choose to work less hours and have more free time. Some will work full time to save for additional schooling or to take long sabbaticals to travel or pursue other interests.

In a society of millionaires, all needs will be met. Prosperity and abundance will abound. Fulfillment will be the norm and quality of life will soar. Eventually, the drive to acquire wealth will fade. With all needs met, money will ultimately become obsolete. We will organically and harmoniously evolve to a moneyless society focused on cultural and individual growth and fulfillment.

The Golden Economy will provide the means for each person to exchange goods and services efficiently in pursuit of individual and societal goals. Its ultimate aspiration is a fulfilling, joyful life for each person. The Golden Economy will create prosperity, wealth and abundance on many levels and enrichment for every member of society.

Growing up in a Republican household as the child of business owners, I heard a great deal about the free market. I heard even more as a finance major in college. The free market was glorified as the solution to all human ills. Indeed, it was deified as the Invisible Hand of the Market that steps in to correct errors and create balance. I bought in to this propaganda for much of my early life, until I could no longer ignore the overwhelming evidence to the contrary. What I was taught in economics class did not mesh with what I learned in history class or what I saw with my own eyes.

A free market supposedly means that all people are free to compete economically on an equal basis. This competition purportedly leads to the highest quality at the lowest price, benefitting all members of society. The message, however, does not equal the reality.

What the free market really means is that those with power and wealth are free to do as they choose, free to manipulate and control the market without interference from the government or from any collective representation of those with less power. Free market means that in the name of personal profit, the ruling class is free to pollute the environment and free to poison the air and water supply. They are free to pay a pittance for 12 to 20 hour work days and free to have children labor in heinous conditions.

The plutocratic definition of free market means lost limbs, burns, injury and death from lack of safety equipment and procedures. It means birth defects, disease and premature death in the general public. It means a toxic environment and extinct species. It means wealth can be used to price products below cost to squeeze smaller competition out of business. It means elections can be manipulated by corporate and business interests through billions of dollars donated to political campaigns. It means speculators can manipulate worthless derivatives, milk the public for billions of dollars, crash the economy and then receive trillions in 'bail outs' from political underlings.

This list may seem awful, but each item on it has occurred and is part of our history under the auspices of the free market. Any changes to the system have been made under extreme duress and often against violent resistance. Power magnates and their propagandists have cried foul at every stage, raging against clean air, clean water, child labor laws, minimum wage laws, occupational safety laws and antitrust laws as violations of the free market. Each of these public protections, they claimed, would harm business and, therefore, be a detriment to society.

The plutocratic elite declare that government should stay out of business and allow the invisible hand of the market to guide affairs. Then, they clamor for trillions in government bailouts when their depredations collapse the market. The free market is not free. Its very name is a propaganda manipulation by those who benefit from economic slavery.

When most people hear the term free market, they really think of a fair market, and that is exactly what I advocate. *A fair market is a market system that allows for the free exchange of goods and services on a fair and equal basis under parameters that protect and benefit every member of society.* A fair market is the system of economic exchange in a truly free society. It creates and supports freedom in ways the so-called free market does not.

Competition is the basis of the free marketeers' argument against rules. They claim rules and regulations limit freedom within the market, causing undue economic hardships and harming competition. Yet, the notion of rules interfering with competition is a fallacy. You can look at any game or sport to see that clearly.

Games and sports are based on competition. Yet, they all have rules that limit and govern behavior. These rules are the bases of the games and are precisely what make them competitive endeavors. Simply put, the games would not exist without the rules. As long as the rules are applied evenly among all participants, competition is fair. Any game or sport can be used as an example to support this principle. I will use football, since it is my favorite.

American football is one of the more popular and profitable professional sports precisely because it is so competitive. Yet, there are far more rules now than there were at its founding over a century ago. These rules have served to make the game more exciting and to increase player safety.

There is far more safety equipment now than ever before. There are regulations governing procedures to be taken in the case of player concussion. There are rules protecting quarterbacks and receivers from being struck in the head. There are also rules designed to increase scoring, making the game more exciting. There are even rules capping the amount of money teams can spend on player salaries so larger market teams don't have unfair financial advantage over the smaller.

As long as they are applied evenly and fairly, these rules ensure the health, popularity, profitability and competitive nature of the game. If all rules were discarded or applied with bias, the game would degenerate quickly. Teams allowed to commit pass interference, for example, would have unfair advantage over others that are not. If safety rules were not applied, the game would become increasingly aggressive and violent. The ruthlessness would spiral until teams intentionally hurt, maim or even kill other players in the effort to win.

This example is not far fetched. Businesses in the current system are more than willing to dump known toxins into the water supply to save costs, increase profits, and give themselves an advantage over their competition. Historically, free market enterprises, in their efforts to maximize gain, have shown consistent willingness to harm individuals, society as a whole, and the environment. As long as profit is the deciding standard by which our market is measured, there will be motivation to choose profit over the well being of others.

Profit remains the ultimate business goal in a fair market, but not at the expense of the health, welfare and lives of the citizenry. Similarly, the goal of a football game is to win, but not at the expense of the lives or well being of the players or fans. If all of the rules of football were discarded, then, technically speaking, one team could shoot the players of the opposing team and win by default.

In football, as with business, competition on a level playing field produces the conditions for the best team to win. Luck is the only other influencing factor. The excitement generated by fair competition attracts fans and the sport remains profitable.

If environmental, labor, safety and financial regulations are applied equally and evenly to all businesses, then the playing field is level and competition is fair. Under these conditions, the most efficiently run businesses generate the most profit. True Capitalists would celebrate a fair market.

Modern 'Propaganda Capitalists' fear a fair market because a level playing field would negate the advantage of their preexisting wealth and force them to compete on an equal basis. The free market is an excuse for licentiousness and abuse of power. The fair market creates fair competition and a level playing field for all.

The free market is based on flawed premises. It assumes that profit is the greatest motivation for human behavior, yet also assumes this motivation will bring about moral and ethical behavior. Their theory is that if a business creates lower prices by behaving immorally, consumers will stop buying from them and the business will fail or have to change its behavior. That is similar to saying if one football team cheats to win, the fans will like the losing teams better, so the team will stop cheating.

While that is very idealistic, it is not at all realistic. What really would happen is that because the team that cheats wins, other teams will begin to cheat as well. Fair play will be gone, cheating will spiral out of control, and the competitive nature of the game will be harmed.

Likewise, if a business achieves lower prices through unethical behavior, consumers, particularly those who are already financially strapped by the current socioeconomic structure, will buy the lower cost goods. Other businesses will duplicate the unethical behavior in order to compete, expanding the downward spiral. The free market actually encourages and rewards negative behavior and harms society as a whole.

There are many motivations for human behavior other than profit. For many people, if not most, financial gain is not the primary motivation in life. Altruism, community well being, self-fulfillment, personal growth, creative satisfaction and a sense of accomplishment are some of the myriad motivations. Most people do not feel a need for ever increasing material gain. They would be satisfied with a comfortable living wage and would prioritize their free time to pursue other interests.

Thus, the free market is dominated by those few for whom profit is the chief motivation. Because profit takes precedence over other priorities, morals and ethics are often discarded and the welfare of society is not taken into consideration. In a fair market, profit and economic expansion are means to achieve societal goals, not ends unto themselves.

WEALTH VS FULFILLMENT

Currently, success is defined by income level and accumulated wealth. We are imprinted with this program. The wealthiest are held in highest regard. Happiness and fulfillment are not taken into consideration. The purpose is not to gain enough wealth to empower and fulfill our dreams. Wealth is seen as an end unto itself. "He who dies with the most toys wins" is the cultural imprint with which we are stamped.

This imprint can be seen in the level of white collar crime. Millionaires and even billionaires are arrested for theft and embezzlement. These people have far more wealth than they will ever need to satisfy every material necessity and every whim they will ever have. Yet, they risk everything and do harm on a wide scale to increase their already vast wealth.

The cultural program tells them that nothing is ever enough and they will be judged by how much they accrue. No matter how much they earn, there is always someone with a bigger house, more cars, a cooler jet and a better yacht. Because of the cultural imprint, no matter how high they climb, it will never be enough. Despite their great success and regardless of how much power and independence they seem to have, they are automatons unconsciously living out their cultural programming.

In a Golden Society, fulfillment will be the criteria for measuring success. Happiness, enrichment and growth will be the socially praiseworthy goals of life. Our heroes will be those who have achieved these, who have pushed the boundaries of knowledge, who have brought benefit to others. The number of countries visited, degrees obtained, instruments played, languages spoken and the amount of love shared and joy brought to others will be status symbols in a heart-based society.

As we shift our concept of success, the pressure to amass inordinate amounts of material wealth will subside. Theft, embezzlement and other financially based crimes will decline and disappear. As material wealth becomes less concentrated, there will be an increase in the general wealth of all citizens. As each person obtains the material means to achieve their goals, society as a whole will attain unprecedented levels of fulfillment, harmony and peace.

There is no problem with illegal drugs. There is no problem with alcohol. The problem is with addiction. Addiction is a disease. Making drugs illegal and criminalizing the associated addictive behavior is tantamount to making pneumonia illegal and imprisoning the people who contract it.

Addiction is also a symptom, a sign that there are deeper issues within an individual. Widespread addiction is a symptom of deeper issues within a society. Addictive behavior is the result of unhappiness, stress, trauma, poverty and hopelessness. A high addiction rate is a sign of societal dysfunction. To acknowledge the source of addictive behavior, the politicians responsible for the function of society would have to acknowledge their failings and press for massive reform. It is far easier and more politically expedient to blame drugs and label the users as criminals.

There is a higher percentage of citizens incarcerated in the U.S. than in any other industrialized country. This is largely due to the war on drugs. According to the Schaffer Library, of the over 1.5 million Americans in federal prison, 59.6% of them are there for drug offenses. That means the lives of over 900,000 Americans are being wasted. This counts only the federal prison population and doesn't include those in state penitentiaries or county jails.

Billions of dollars are squandered each year on investigation, prosecution and imprisonment of drug offenders. Families are torn apart, productivity is diminished, violent and property crimes increase, and lives are lost.

If legal, most recreational drugs would be rather inexpensive. Current price levels are due to legal machinations. Almost everyone is familiar with the supply and demand curves. When supply is artificially decreased, the curve shifts and prices are artificially inflated. Drug criminalization laws drastically shift the curve, inflating prices tremendously. Due to these higher prices, theft increases as a means for the poor to pay for their supply. ·

Just as with prohibition in the 1920s, the artificially high value of a relatively small quantity breeds violence for control and ownership of the trade. In the case of alcohol, once prohibition ended, related gang violence ceased. There was no more profit in black market trade. You no longer see organized crime families going to war over truckloads of beer or whiskey. If personal drugs were legal, there would be no more violence associated with them.

I find it fascinating to observe how much money beer and liquor companies donate to anti-drug campaigns. Don't mistake this for altruism and care for social well being. It is a means to keep low priced competition out of the market.

Addiction takes many forms. By falsely identifying drugs and alcohol as the problem, addiction as a disease is ignored. Some addictions are normalized or even praised. Addiction to gambling, shopping, sex, eating, money and power are all destructive manifestations of the same addictive behavior. But, these are more socially accepted and, therefore, legal. In the cases of addiction to money and power, the resultant wealth is praised and idealized.

The focus should not be on the symptoms or the categories of addictive behavior. It should be on curing addictive behavior in any form and reforming the social pressures that are the root of the behavior. Fortunately, in a Golden Society, the solution is once again simple and interconnected with all other solutions.

Legalize personal drug use and provide rehabilitation for those who wish to break and heal their addiction. Release all prisoners who have been convicted of nonviolent drug offenses. This step alone will save billions of dollars annually which can be applied to more beneficial sectors of society. Total annual prison expenditures, including state, federal and private prisons, add up to over $40

Billion per year. $20 to $25 Billion of that goes to imprisonment for drug related crimes. Imagine how much education and health care can be provided for $20 Billion per year.

Closing the DEA alone will save over $2 Billion per year. Closing all other drug related law enforcement units will save over $5 Billion more. Not only can this money be diverted to more useful purposes, but the remaining law enforcement assets will be freed to concentrate on crimes that actually are a detriment to society. There truly is more than enough money to fund a Golden Society if we spend it wisely.

With personal drugs going from the black market to being sold openly on the fair market, taxes can be charged. Instead of a drain on society's resources, the sale of personal drugs will bring revenue. As discussed in the chapter on tax reform, a surtax can be added, netting billions in revenue. This will fund rehabilitation as well as compensate wellness mutuals for the additional health costs associated with personal drug use.

I have seen many people break many addictions and have seen many others remain dependent. Those who broke out had one thing in common. They all decided to change. If a person is not ready to break their addiction, no amount of punishment, shame, imprisonment, rehabilitation or counseling will make a difference. Attempting to force change by punishing people for their addiction only increases their stress and drives them further into addiction.

People will change only when they are ready. Rehabilitation facilities should be available for when that time comes. Sometimes addicts have to hit bottom before they are ready to change. Though well intentioned, preventing them from hitting bottom is a disservice to their recovery.

Addicts should be left to their devices as long as they are not disturbing or endangering others with their behavior. As with alcohol, drug use should be confined to private homes and designated public areas. Driving or any other activity in which impairment increases risk to others should be forbidden. Everyone has the right to make choices concerning their own lives, but they do not have the right to cause undue danger to others.

115

The transition to a Golden Society will eliminate the dysfunction that is the stimulus for most addictive behavior. The end of poverty, increased fulfillment, improved wellness care, healthy diet, clean water, universal education, and renewed hope will all contribute to a much more emotionally and mentally healthy population. Simply put, a healthier, happier society will not be as susceptible to the dangers of addictive behavior.

Once societal stimuli for addiction have been removed and rehabilitation services have been provided, personal drugs will only be used for recreational and ceremonial purposes. Educated sovereign individuals have the right to choose as they may, provided they bring no undue harm to others. If they wish to explore or enjoy a certain type of experience, it is not the place of another to judge them morally.

Over time, as the joys of living from the heart in a Golden Society take root, the impetus for drug use will decline. Eventually, it will dwindle to the point that it is a non-issue and ultimately will cease altogether.

CHAPTER 13
CRIME AND PUNISHMENT

"*As above, so below.*" The current system of crime and punishment is a microcosm of society's current religious imprint of the macrocosm. The prevailing belief is that good people go to Heaven and bad people go to Hell. The modern criminal justice system is a temporal reflection of that imprinted belief.

Good people go free, bad people go to prison. Bad people do bad things and deserve to be punished. Little thought is given to rehabilitation. It is very black and white with little allowance for the potential to change or understanding of cause and effect.

In a Golden Society, understanding of the nature and purpose of Life will be applied to the criminal justice system. Life is about growth and evolution. Beings are not born evil, only undeveloped and in need of education. People on a path of learning and growth, by definition, can not be expected to know everything. Cause and effect must be taken into account.

Undeveloped beings are far more likely to commit crimes, particularly those beings who have been exposed to violent or abusive behavior as children, and those living without hope of escape from poverty. The character of a Golden Society will remove most of the stimuli for most crimes. We have already discussed reform in drug policy. This reform alone will decriminalize almost 60% of the federal prison population.

MONETARY CRIME

Eliminating poverty and instituting universal education, easier financial conditions and a shift in societal focus from wealth accumulation to personal fulfillment will reduce the pressures and incentives

117

for monetary based crimes. According to the Shaffer Library, just over 23% of federal inmates are monetary offenders (robbery, property crimes, extortion, fraud, bribery and other white collar crimes). Many of these crimes will be eliminated of their own accord with the change in financial and social conditions. Most of the remainder can be rehabilitated effectively.

Around 80% of current crime can be eliminated by enacting the changes in drug policy and the economic, education and other reforms proposed here. It should be relatively easy to rehabilitate the few remaining monetary criminals, particularly the poverty based crimes. If a white collar criminal embezzles millions to line his pockets, that is one thing. If someone steals to buy food or pay for medicine, it is altogether different.

In the case of white collar crime, the best way to modify this behavior and to deter future crime is to force repayment of the stolen money. The entire motivation for the crime is to increase wealth. If stolen wealth must be repaid with interest and penalty, the net effect will be a reduction in the wealth of the criminal. If the stolen wealth has been spent or hidden, then the criminal's assets can be forfeit to repay the debt. If this is still insufficient, future earnings can be heavily garnished until the debt is fully repaid.

Counseling can be provided to help white collar criminals shift their focus from wealth accumulation and reprogram their psyches to focus on personal growth, fulfillment and quality of life. This change in focus will help heal the root cause of the criminal behavior.

These are far more effective remedies than paying to imprison white collar criminals in minimum security prisons, eventually releasing them to enjoy the fruits of their crimes. If the goal of the crime is to increase wealth, but the result is decreased wealth, future crimes will be effectively deterred. Penalty charges can be used to defray the cost of investigation and prosecution of the crime, easing the strain on the justice system and freeing resources for other uses.

In the case of poverty based monetary and property crimes, the poverty must be solved. In a Golden Society, there will be means for people to raise themselves from poverty. If some people do not avail themselves of these opportunities, either through ignorance or choice, then a program of poverty rehabilitation should be established for them.

The current criminal justice system imprisons poverty criminals as punishment and to exact a social penance. Little if any effort is put into solving the crisis of poverty. Convicts are released after an arbitrary period of time with reduced chances of finding gainful employment due to their criminal records.

In a Golden Society, the purpose of sentencing will be to create changes in awareness and behavior, permanently solving the situation. While imprisoned to prevent further danger to society, inmates should undergo counseling and testing to determine the reason for their crimes. If poverty was the root cause, the reason for the poverty should be determined.

Generally, these individuals will lack education and employable skills and may also suffer from emotional and/or mental disorders. While incarcerated in a rehabilitation facility, the inmate should receive General and Initial Career Education. Emotional and mental therapy should be provided as well until it is determined that a necessary level of functionality has been attained. Further counseling and therapy may be required after release, but that can be provided privately through insurance mutuals.

Once an inmate has completed Initial Career Education, job placement services should be provided. The inmate can enter a job search and work release program. Such a program will allow him to leave the rehabilitation facility during the day in search of work while returning at night. If the rehabilitation facility is not close enough to his home or to available work, he can be transferred to one that is. Once the inmate is gainfully employed, he can be fully released from the facility. Follow up counseling should continue for some time after release to ensure successful integration into society and to prevent future problems before they occur.

Rehabilitation facilities should be places of work. Private industry and agriculture can associate with rehabilitation facilities. Reduced costs or other considerations can be exchanged for assisting the rehabilitation process. Care should be taken that these businesses do not gain an unfair advantage over other businesses, thus creating imbalance in the fair market. Extreme care should also be taken to ensure the prisoners receive a fair wage and are not exploited. In a heart-based society, oversight should be a straightforward affair.

When not studying or undergoing counseling, inmates can work at an associated industry. Their pay can be divided between defraying the cost of their confinement, recompensing the victims of their crimes, and saving to have a fund available at the time of their release. This system will reduce the cost of rehabilitation, facilitate integration into society and financially compensate victims. If the victims have not been fully compensated by the time the inmate's rehabilitation is complete, future wages above poverty level can be garnished just as with the General Assistance Fund.

This heart-based solution has many benefits. The root causes of the crimes will be addressed. Repeat offenses will be minimized. Victims will be compensated. Cost of rehabilitation will be partially defrayed. Citizens who were previously drains on society's resources will be converted to productive, functional, tax paying members of society. The quality of life and fulfillment of the offenders will increase, increasing the overall wellness of society as a whole.

There are some monetary based offenders who commit crimes by choice. They are drawn by the thrill of the crime, the lure of easy money or other factors. Some people, due to emotional issues or for other reasons, will refuse to cooperate with rehabilitation efforts. In such cases, the offenders must remain detained until they have a change of heart. As with addiction, change cannot be forced. No one will do so until they are ready and decide for themselves.

VIOLENT CRIME

Just over 11% of crime is violent or related to violence (Violent-2.7%, Firearms, Explosives and Arson-8.6%). Addressing these will be a major concern in our new society. Studies have proven that virtually all violent offenders, well over 90%, were exposed to violence or were victims of violence at a young age. This includes sex offenders, who were almost universally molested as children. The theory that some people are 'born bad' just doesn't cut it. Violent offenders are made, not born.

The policies of a Golden Society will remove the pressures that lead to most crimes, but a special effort must be made to break the cycle of violence. During General Education, educators must observe children for signs that they are being exposed to violence and abuse. Such cases should be investigated thoroughly. Those discovered to be victims of violence should receive comprehensive counseling and therapy for as long as it takes to heal the emotional wounds fully. Most violent behavior can be eliminated within one generation by nipping it in the bud, so to speak. By healing the wounds caused by violent behavior, the cycle can be successfully broken.

Currently, violent crime is treated as though there is an inherent 'badness' in the perpetrator. They are seen as knowing better but choosing to do wrong. As such, they are imprisoned as punishment. When the punishment period is complete, the offender is released. It is hoped that he learned the lesson that crime doesn't pay and will fear to commit future crimes. Yet, the root cause of the crime has not been addressed and the motivation still exists within the criminal. Chances are high that the crime will be repeated.

Those who perpetrate violent crime are wounded themselves and need healing. Most can be rehabilitated. They do need to be imprisoned, not as punishment or as a form of collective revenge, but to protect others from further violence as long as the inmate poses a danger to society. Release from prison should not be based on an arbitrary time frame, but on whether the perpetrator has achieved real healing and whether the emotional stimulus to commit violent crime has been successfully addressed.

Violence committed against a child indelibly imprints its young, vulnerable emotional body. Unless extensive, effective treatment is received, the imprint remains into adulthood, affecting the person throughout its life. Even though they consciously may know better, these victims are often subconsciously driven to violent acts as their emotional bodies try to work through the effects of the violence that was done to them. No amount of punishment will cure the emotional wounding done to them or prevent the unconscious urges those wounds engender.

It is easy to use these people as scapegoats and to exact retribution and revenge, but this doesn't solve the problem. Violent offenders should be seen for the sicknesses they have. Just as with infectious diseases, they need to be quarantined from the general population until the illness has been healed.

There should be special facilities for violent offenders. This will keep nonviolent inmates safe while facilitating the specialized treatment needed by violent offenders. Therapists and rehabilitation experts should design treatment programs on individual bases based on each unique situation. As rehabilitation takes effect and an inmate becomes healthier by degrees, his freedom within the facility can increase. Ultimately, the therapists and rehabilitation experts will determine if and when an inmate is healed and no longer a threat of violent behavior. Only then, can he be eligible for release and return to public life.

In some cases, the psychological damage may be so great that the inmate can never be freed. Certain people may show no remorse or may refuse to cooperate with therapy. Some may have suffered so much emotional harm that there is no way they can ever be cured to the point that they would be safe in the general population. In such cases, we must be prepared to incarcerate the offender for life in a humane, but extremely secure, facility.

END PRIVATE PRISONS

Private prisons are a blot on our society. It is unconscionable to profit from the incarceration of others. Nevertheless, private prisons are one of the faster growing segments of the current economy.

When there is a profit motive connected to the criminal justice system, the temptations for corruption and profiteering are too great. There have already been cases of corrupt judges increasing conviction rates and convicting innocent people in exchange for kickbacks from prison corporations.

When profit is based on the number of prisoners in the system, there is incentive to increase and maintain that number. I am firmly convinced that is a major reason for the current drug policy. Imagine how much income the 900,000 federally incarcerated drug offenders mean to prison corporations. At approximately $25,000 per prisoner per year, the amount is over $22.5 Billion. That is more than enough financial incentive to manipulate the system.

Private prison corporations spend millions to lobby Congress and contribute millions more to political campaigns in order to buy influence. Laws are made to benefit prison corporations and increase the prison population. It is no wonder there is a higher percentage of Americans in prison than any other major country. Does anyone really believe American citizens are inherently more criminal than the rest of the world?

There is more profit in keeping someone in prison and in creating repeat offenders than there is in rehabilitation and creating productive citizens. This is another example of how free market based profit motive does not serve the interests of society. Until prisons are removed from the hands of private corporations, there can be no justice in the justice system.

Total prison spending is currently over $40 Billion per year. When initiation of a Golden Society reduces the prison population by 90% through the institution of the measures presented in this chapter, the savings will be over $36 Billion annually. How much good can we do with $36 Billion per year? How many educations can be provided? How many wellness care policies can be assisted? How many people can be permanently raised out of poverty?

Creating a fair and functional justice system is really just a matter of common sense and integrity combined with a clear understanding of human nature. The transition to a Golden Society will, in the space of one generation, reduce crime to less than 10% of its current levels, moving quickly toward the ultimate goal of a crime free society. In that time, trillions of dollars will be saved, not to mention the tragic waste of human potential that will be averted. The resulting increased productivity, fulfillment and quality of life cannot be valued in dollars.

Many people on a path of spiritual self-awareness shun the military. These people seek a way of peace and harmony and abhor violence in any form. Their perspective is understandable, yet they are missing part of the larger picture.

One of my spiritual mentors often said, *"To go beyond a certain point in Creation, you must be a Warrior."* Warrior qualities such as courage, daring, discipline, mental toughness, persistence, focus and dedication are absolutely necessary on a spiritual path. He would also say, *"The greatest battle you will ever fight is for control of your own soul."* As you proceed through the levels of Creation, you will find many beings who desire to control you. Earth isn't the only place where this happens. You must be ready to stand up for your freedom and independence, regardless of what it takes.

Protecting your integrity doesn't mean that you seek violence or revel in it. It means you seek peace and personal sovereignty and are willing to pay the price. My favorite historical examples of this ethos are Taoist monks and Shaolin priests. Few people would accuse them of seeking violence or being of a violent nature, but they have the ability to defend themselves as they follow their paths of personal growth.

Supernovas destroy entire solar systems. Galaxies collide and rip one another apart. Volcanos erupt. The Earth quakes. Nature is violent on a daily basis in ways more powerful than man can imagine. Yet, no one is offended or morally outraged. Violence is a part of Life. It is part of Creation.

The issue is not violence. The concern should be unsolicited control of other sentient beings. Violence is only one of many tools used to that end. Restriction of a human being's right to self-determination is the greatest of all violations. The right to self-determination should be your focus, not violence.

Understand this very clearly. ***You have the right to Be YourSelf.*** You were born with that right. It cannot be taken from you. It can only be violated. You have the inherent right to use as much force as necessary to defend your freedom from any person, group, government or organization who would violate your right to self-determination. You were born to Be YourSelf. Anyone who interferes with that is interfering with the purpose behind your Creation. They are interfering with the Will of the Creator.

I encourage anyone on a path of spiritual self-awareness who is prejudiced against violence to take martial arts classes. Martial arts is a healthy way of exploring your personal perception of violence and becoming comfortable with that aspect of Creation. To understand Life truly, if something repels you, move closer to it. Explore it, get to know it until you can see that it, too, is a legitimate part of Creation. To become Whole, you must open yourself to all aspects of Life until you can see that All comes from the same Source.

TRUE WARRIORS

The highest expressions of a third or fourth dimensional society are its artists and its Warriors. Its artists stretch the creative boundaries and are the driving force of growth. Its warriors protect it and keep it safe. By warriors, I am not referring to teenage recruits that are used by the power elite as cannon fodder for the war industry. Warriors are those beings born with higher levels of intelligence, psychological stability and physical constitution who dedicate their abilities to the protection of defenseless individuals and society as a whole.

In the past, warrior-poets such as the samurai were not only warriors, calligraphers, and poets, but were also expected to live by a higher standard of behavior and ethics. In modern times, these warriors can be found in Delta Force, SEAL Teams and other Special

126

Operations Forces as well as some career officers and NCO's in conventional units.

My concern for them is that, with warfare becoming an industry and with so many conflicts motivated by banking and corporate interests, the special forces have been expanded rapidly and vast sums of money have been put at their disposal. Under these circumstances, lower standards are a temptation and corruption is a danger.

WAR AS CONTROL

Just as an individual has the right and responsibility to defend him or herself, so too does a society. As long as we exist in a world of polarities, there will be the need for self-defense to maintain personal and political sovereignty. But, threat assessment and self-defense needs must be based on reality. Most of the 'threats' today are contrived by the propaganda machine of the ruling elite and designed to create fear for the purpose of increased social control.

To the U.S. homeland, there is very little danger of external aggression. The threats that do exist are deliberately blown out of proportion. The remainder are intentionally fabricated to generate fear. People in fear desire protection. They are willing to surrender money, resources and even their rights and freedoms in an effort to stay safe. The power brokers methodically create false threats to convince the populace by degrees to surrender their personal sovereignty and financial resources.

War is big business. Bombs and bandages are expensive. Trillions are spent on defense budgets. U.S. Defense spending is over $600 Billion annually, not counting emergency appropriations for war funding. The war industry has grown fat manufacturing weapons, ammunition and supplies, but that isn't the real power and profit in the defense game.

Wars cost more money than governments have available. The difference must be borrowed. Since their survival is at stake, nations are willing to borrow any sum necessary under almost any terms. Warring nations go into debt to bankers and are thereafter at their mercy. Throughout history, there are many instances of members of the same banking houses loaning money to both sides of a war.

There are also occasions in which the roots of war can be traced to banking institutions manipulating events to increase their profit and influence.

The winner and loser of a war can be decided by control of the money supply. If you can't buy guns and ammunition, you can't fight. Thus, the bankers are really in control. They, along with the manufacturers of war materiel, are the only real winners. The primary outcome of most wars is that all nations involved end up deep in debt and beholden to banking interests. Debt often increases even more after the end of a war as money must be borrowed to rebuild.

THE CALL OF THE WARRIOR

As a young man, I felt the call of the Warrior. Unaware of the internal spiritual connection, I externalized the call and joined the Army. I was patriotic and idealistic and I loved being a soldier. I loved the hard work, the camaraderie, the challenge, the esprit de corps, and the sense of contribution to a greater good. I was wholly willing to fight and die for my country and for the cause of freedom.

Over time, as meditation opened my mind and my eyes, I saw the deceptions and falsehoods inherent in the system. I realized I had been sold a lie. Disillusionment soon followed. I came to understand that I was not training to fight for my country or for freedom, but for the interests of bankers and corporations. The oath I swore as an enlisted man and again as an officer was to *"support and defend the Constitution of the United States of America against all enemies, foreign and domestic."* I realized that the greatest threat to the Constitution was from our own government and from the banking and corporate masters that manipulate it, so I left the Army.

I understood that the only real way to fulfill my oath would be to restore Constitutional government and human rights and freedoms. I dedicated my life to that purpose. This book is the result of my efforts. It describes the revolution in awareness necessary to achieve a revolution in our reality.

By the time I left the Army, I better understood the warrior ethic and I applied it to my internal spiritual journey. It has served me well. I have lived some fine adventures, had many amazing experiences, and learned more than my mind could have imagined. Experience has shown me that the Cosmos is vastly sublime and we have our rightful place in it. There is no limit to human spiritual potential.

REVEILLE

I feel for my brothers and sisters in arms who joined the military with similar idealism and patriotism only to find themselves betrayed. Many don't even realize yet that they are being manipulated and that their lives and health are being risked to increase the power of an elite that benefits from the business of war.

Domestic discontent with the current socioeconomic system is growing and the people are beginning to stand up for their rights and freedoms. Protests will grow in size and strength. I hope the eyes of my brothers and sisters in arms open to reality before the time comes that they are ordered to fire on their own people.

THREAT ASSESSMENT

The establishment puts a great deal of energy into scaring you in order to justify the freedoms they restrict and the trillions they request to 'keep you safe.' In truth, the threat to the homeland is minimal if not nonexistent.

Think about it. A conventional military attack on the continental United States is virtually impossible. We sit on a vast island between two vast oceans. To invade the U.S., troops, equipment and materials would have to be moved across an ocean under constant attack from naval and air forces. A landing would have to be made, a beachhead secured, and territory conquered against the resistance of an entire population. Resupply and reinforcements would have to come across that same ocean.

It cannot be done. There are not enough troops and ships in the entire world to carry off such an enterprise. Any enemy determined to do so would have to spend years and trillions of dollars to manufacture enough tanks, planes and ships. Not only would the effort bankrupt them, it could not be hidden. There would be advance warning in plenty of time to prepare.

So, if there is no direct threat to the homeland, why do we have such a massive military? Might it be to protect corporate and banking interests around the world? How much is spent protecting oil fields and shipping lanes? Now that we understand the reality of free energy and the hoax of the energy industry, we know that the military is really being used to protect the monopoly of a false industry whose sole purpose is to bleed our wealth. Instead of protecting the people, our military is being used as a tool to fleece and steal from those very people.

With conventional threats disproven, only nuclear and terrorism remain. The Cold War has ended. The nuclear threat from the Soviet Union is gone. The U.S. still has enough nuclear firepower to destroy all life on Earth several times. No sovereign nation-state, no matter how rogue, is suicidal enough to launch a nuclear attack on our homeland. Retaliation would be swift and unthinkably brutal.

Current propaganda efforts would have us wring our hands in fear over smaller nations obtaining nuclear capability. The fact remains that those nations would not dare to use nuclear weapons to attack the U.S. homeland. They want nuclear weapons for self-defense.

Tactical nuclear weapons are a means for smaller nations to defend themselves against stronger powers. If a small country were to be invaded by a more powerful nation, a tactical nuclear weapon could be used to destroy the invading army. The weaker nation's ability to defend itself with tactical nuclear weapons eliminates the advantage of the more powerful nation and levels the playing field rather rapidly.

The bankers and corporate manipulators use the U.S. military as a club to keep their pawns in line. If an invading army can be destroyed with a tactical nuclear weapon, the bankers lose their club and their ability to bully the weak. The bankers' control is threatened by tactical nuclear weapons in the hands of small nations. The U.S. homeland is not. The nuclear threat from sovereign nation states is not real. It is fear propaganda.

The final 'threat' is terrorism. Fear mongering propaganda would have you believe that terrorists hate the U.S. because they hate freedom and prosperity. This is ridiculous. They resent interventionist U.S. policies supporting banker and corporate greed.

The International Monetary Fund and the World Bank work with U.S. corporations and banks to manipulate nations to strip them of their resources. Third world countries are left destitute. Their their citizens are impoverished and their natural environments are devastated, while these private institutions grow ever wealthier and more powerful.

The U.S. military, stationed in over 700 bases in more than 130 countries, has become the enforcement arm of what is essentially an organized crime syndicate. American bases on foreign soil in and of themselves are sources of discontent. Even more so is their use to enforce greed and corruption. Is it any wonder that resentment is fostered or that people without other means of resistance would choose terrorism as their method? What would U.S. citizens do if the situation was reversed? How far would you go to defend your home and family?

Government policies and the policies of those that control the government are the source of the discontent that leads to terrorism. Terrorism is then used as propaganda by the power elite to generate fear in the U.S. population. This fear is used as an excuse to increase defense spending and to further aggressive policies, which in turn foster greater resentment and more violent reprisals. An ever expanding cycle is created, increasing the profit, power and control of the elite.

There is actually greater danger of the banker controlled cabal engineering a false flag terrorist or nuclear attack than there is of a real attack by a terrorist organization or a rogue nation. The power elite has a great deal more to gain from such an attack than any third world nation or terrorist organization.

The common sense policy changes that will occur in a Golden Society will eliminate the motivation for terrorism. By eradicating corruption, greed and interventionism, the grievances driving terrorism will be dispelled. A person has to be extremely discontented, desperate and disillusioned to be convinced to strap a bomb to his body and blow himself up. It won't take much to convince him otherwise.

Conventional and nuclear threats to the U.S homeland are minimal or nonexistent. Terrorism is intentionally contrived and can be eliminated. In a Golden Society, the sole purpose of the military will be the protection of the homeland, its citizens, and human rights. With this in mind, we can rethink and restructure our armed forces.

RESTRUCTURING

In 2010, U.S. military expenditures were $687.1 Billion. That was 43% of the entire world's 2010 military spending. The U.S. spent more on defense than the next 20 highest military spenders combined. The closest nation was China who spent $114.3 Billion. That was one-sixth of the amount spent by the U.S. Does our defense really cost over 6 times that of any other country? Do we need to spend more money than 20 other nations combined in order to be safe? Are we really that hated? Are we in that much danger? If so, why?

We are not in that much danger and, despite our policies, we are not that hated. It is quite clear from these numbers that the U.S. military is not tasked with the defense of the U.S. The U.S. armed forces are the worldwide enforcement arm of the banking and corporate interests that manipulate world politics and the world economy.

U.S. military spending can be cut to one-fourth of current levels, to $171 Billion, and still remain 50% greater than the next closest nation. We would be absolutely safe spending far less than that. If Canada and European nations can protect themselves by spending only $20 Billion to $60 Billion, why can't the U.S. be safe spending $171 Billion?

Using 2010 numbers, if we cut three-fourths from the military budget, we would save over $515 Billion. This does not mean cuts in spending for Veterans Affairs or for Homeland Security, which is the agency responsible for guarding against terrorism. Those are separate budgets.

That $515 Billion in savings, when added to savings on the interest on the national debt, prison reform and other savings, combines to over $1 Trillion. Universal education and wellness care can be immediate realities. There are more than enough resources and money. Over time, as the benefits of a Golden Society take effect, military spending can be further reduced and that money can also be put to use more beneficially.

Foreign bases can be closed along with many domestic bases. Property from closed bases can be sold and the proceeds can be prorated into the budget. Troops and equipment can be brought home. Many troops can be discharged. Equipment can be stored and maintained against the day it may someday be needed. Reserve forces can be trained and returned to their civilian lives to be available in the event of a true foreign threat. Professional soldiers can be maintained on active duty as a cadre to train recruits, should rapid expansion be necessary.

Active air and submarine forces would be effective protection against foreign invasion. Other naval forces can be maintained to protect shipping lanes and guard against piracy. Nuclear forces can be maintained as a deterrent until all nations agree to total nuclear disarmament. Great diplomatic effort should be spent in that direction.

The U.S. would be safer under this plan than in its current state of massive military spending. The fiscal savings would make the nation stronger economically, providing the financial base to arm itself in the unlikely event that military expansion would be needed in the future.

FREEDOM CORPS

In a Golden Society, the only military unit dedicated to operating on foreign soil will be the Freedom Corps. This all volunteer force will be dedicated to humanitarian aid. True Warriors would flock to this banner, desiring to use their skill to help those in need. These would be highly motivated, highly trained and well equipped units that specialize not only in combat, but in engineering, medicine and societal infrastructure.

Famine victims can be aided and food and medicine protected. Immediate assistance can be rendered to victims of natural disasters. Mobile hospitals, water pumping and purification facilities, power generation stations and sanitation facilities can be set up and guarded. Public security can be provided until stability is restored.

In cases of genocide and grievous human rights abuses, dictators can and should be overthrown. Professional soldiers and true Warriors would jump at the chance to stop atrocities and bring peace. The genocide, ethnic cleansing, and human rights abuses that occurred in Rwanda, the Balkans and elsewhere would not be tolerated by a Golden Society.

Leadership is a sacred responsibility. A leader has the duty and responsibility to guide his or her people to healthy, productive, fulfilling lives. Any leader who abuses power, abuses human rights, and, especially, who commits genocide forfeits his right to remain in a position of leadership. Such leaders can rightfully be removed from power and made to answer for their crimes.

The Freedom Corps must be an all volunteer force. Their purview would extend beyond the defense of the homeland and protection of U.S. citizens. If they are to go into harm's way for any other reason, it must be by choice. Most Warriors would be gratified to defend the weak and defenseless. There will be no shortage of volunteers. But, it must be their decision since it is their lives that will be at stake.

In all cases, it should be determined that they have the support of the local population before going to assist. Every effort should be made to work with local leaders. Ensuring the cooperation of the general public has been a basic military principle since the time of Sun Tzu.

After some dictators have been removed from power and brought to justice, the remainder will think twice before committing atrocities and human rights abuses. Peace and justice can be created and maintained without resorting to military action.

FOREIGN POLICY

Foreign policy in a Golden Society will be based on one factor: human rights. There is no other factor that matters. A universal standard for human rights should be set forth. The U.N. Declaration of Human Rights is a good start. Wage and environmental protections need to be considered as well.

Any nation committed to the principles of human rights can exchange with a Golden Society on an equal basis. Citizens can pass freely across borders and international trade can be conducted free of tariffs and duties.

Nations that violate human rights principles will engender varying degrees of foreign policy restrictions. If, in an effort to gain an economic advantage, a nation does not comply with environmental, wage, or human rights standards, then that nation shall incur tariffs and duties calculated to nullify that advantage and to act as additional disincentive.

For example, a nation disregards certain environmental standards to reduce manufacturing costs. Those savings are calculated to be 20%. A 20% tariff would be added to imports from that country to keep the market fair and to level the playing field with businesses from nations that do hold to the standards. An additional amount can be added as a disincentive to help convince that country to change its policies.

Trade may take place with countries that commit minor human rights violations. Tariffs will be added as protest against these violations and as disincentive for continued abuse. Hopefully, these countries will choose to change their policies as they experience diminished profits while other countries reap the benefits of free trade and human rights.

No country should be cut off completely from international trade. At the very least, trade of food and medicine will keep lines of communication open while providing for humanitarian needs.

One of the more poorly considered foreign policies in our history was the decision to cut off North Korea completely from trade, including food and medicine. The objective was for the extreme unrelieved poverty to foment discontent and revolution in the North Korean people. The policy failed utterly.

North Koreans were so poor and so desperate that many were reduced to boiling grass for food. Other than in a few cities, there was no electricity for heat or lighting. Yet, because of their forced isolation, North Korean peasants assumed that the entire world lived under the same conditions. Thus, the isolation policy backfired. Its only result was to exacerbate the suffering of the North Korean people.

If food and medicine had been provided, the North Korean citizens would have known that other countries had surpluses of these products. There would have been cross-cultural contact as the supplies were delivered. Eventually, the North Koreans would have come to understand the failings of their leadership and would have demanded change. Not only would providing humanitarian aid have been the compassionate thing to do, it would have eventually led to the North Korean citizens seeking freedom and a change in government.

Diplomacy and foreign policy in a Golden Society will be straightforward affairs. There will be no need for political machinations and geopolitics. Human rights will be the standard. All countries will be dealt with evenly. Eventually, all nations will realize the benefit of granting full human rights to their citizens and will join the world community of free peoples. When that happens, the need for military spending to guard against terrestrial threats will cease. Peace and prosperity for all will be the prize!

In an ideal future, there will be no threat of violence or external control, and there will be no need for military or defense forces. Forming a Golden Society is a great leap in that direction. Until that day arrives, our decisions must be based on a realistic assessment of the situation.

CHAPTER 15
WORLD UNITY GOVERNMENT

The idea of a world government makes many people nervous, with very good reason. The term 'world government' conjures up images of the New World Order. The power elite has been manipulating events in that direction for quite some time. They seek a world dictatorship, or at least a police state officially governed by a plutocracy. Their endgame is to unite the entire world under their power and control.

The opposite polarity of this concept is a world unity government based on freedom and human rights guaranteed for each individual. A Golden Society is a society of the heart. It understands the inter-connectedness of all Life. It recognizes that we are all One and that what happens to any individual affects the Whole. With the aware-ness of our Oneness rising to the forefront of human consciousness, it only makes sense that it will be expressed through unification.

As humanity enters a new aeon, we will inevitably move into a unified form of government. The question is, which polarity will that take? Will we move gracefully, intentionally and consciously into a global expression of human unity, or will we be forcefully compelled into a totalitarian slave state? We really do have a choice. The so-called New World Order has its blueprint in place. Now the positive polarity of love, freedom and fulfillment has a blueprint for the other potential.

Unity does not mean uniformity. Unity is an expression of the Oneness that we share. Its basis is in diverse individuality. The only characteristic that we each truly have in common is that we are all different, all unique, all individuals.

Our individuality is the building block of our society. Every part of this blueprint has been focused on empowering each individual to find and develop his or her own unique inner essence. Embodying and expanding the True Self is the purpose of Life, and thus is the basis for a Golden Society.

The purpose of government is to provide common goods for the common good. Protection and assurance of individual rights is by far the most significant common good provided by a Golden government. This is as true for a world government as it is for individual nations.

When individual rights are guaranteed, there is no need to fight for specialized rights. There will be no need for women's rights, gay rights, ethnic rights, racial rights, religious rights or any other form of specialized rights. All will be guaranteed as individual rights.

Make no mistake, I am not talking about democracy here. Democracy is rule of the people, or, by some translations, rule of the mob. The Golden world government will be based on rule of the individual. Democratic principles will be involved, but must remain subservient to individual rights.

In a Golden Society, the population will be more highly educated, more highly aware and have more heart consciousness than ever before. Nevertheless, there still exists the possibility that, in a moment of extreme emotion, the majority will vote away the rights of individuals or of a minority. This must be prevented. Absolute guarantee of individual human rights is the means.

A Golden world government can provide common goods for the common good while preserving cultural diversity, regional uniqueness and individual sovereignty. Masai rituals, Bavarian biergartens and Chinese sampans will be equally treasured as diverse expressions of human culture. A unity government will facilitate cultural exchange while preserving cultural distinctiveness.

Free energy, clean water, healthy food, wellness care and universal education are common needs of every individual. A fair and just common currency issued by the people's representatives will facilitate trade, travel and economic growth.

A Golden Society is based on reality, on the Laws of Creation and the purpose of Life. Because I was born in the United States, I have written this book from the perspective of a U.S. citizen. Yet, these principles can be applied to any nation on Earth. The movement can begin anywhere. Who will be first? As individual nations adopt these principles, they will thrive and their citizens will flourish. Other nations will witness this prosperity and will choose to adopt the principles as well. Golden Society will spread organically and naturally across the globe.

As ever more nations embrace Golden Society, there will be a movement to unify under a single banner. Two or more bold and enterprising nations will eventually choose to work together to codify individual human rights and to harmonize education, wellness care, food supply, energy, monetary and tax systems.

Once a successful merger has been accomplished, a template will exist. It will then be easier for other nations to take that step in the future. Momentum will build. As more nations transition to Golden Society, their prosperity and fulfillment will motivate ever more nations to follow suit. As unified nations prosper, other nations will choose to unify with them as well.

The transition to a world unity government can happen organically, naturally and voluntarily. As the truth emerges, others will wish to join in. The momentum will generate a positive feedback loop and the revolution will spiral outward until it encompasses all.

Humanity is entering a new era. A world government is going to happen. The only questions involve how and what form it will take. The answers will be determined by a collective choice between fear and love. A Golden Society is based on living from the heart. It is a society of Love. Here is the blueprint to manifest that choice. We can make it happen!

"Good government never depends upon laws, but upon the personal qualities of those who govern. The machinery of government is always subordinate to the will of those who administer that machinery. The most important element of government, therefore, is the method of choosing leaders."

FROM *CHILDREN OF DUNE*, BY FRANK HERBERT

Ultimately and ideally, a Golden Society will be governed by what I call a Sophiacracy, rule of the Wise, from the ancient Greek *Sophia* meaning Wisdom and *kratos* meaning rule or power. Since the purpose of life is growth, and the general population of a Golden Society lives in their hearts, it stands to reason that those who guide and lead the people must exist at a higher level than the heart. Wisdom comes from the Crown chakra. The principle consciousness of those who rule should exist in their Crown or in even higher levels of their Beings.

When the Crown chakra opens, an extra-dimensional golden glow radiates from the third ventricle of the brain. This glow can be seen with the inner vision. It is the source of the halo image seen around the heads of saints in mystical and religious paintings. That halo exists about the heads of the Wise and is very real.

This halo or Golden Crown is an indication of the divine awareness resulting from the opening of the Crown chakra. This awareness was the original source of the concept of the divine right to rule. In ancient days, there literally were priest-kings, yogi-kings and god-kings (and queens). These were Crown consciousness beings whose duty was to rule with Divine Wisdom, progressing the masses through the School of Life to better lives, more advanced understandings, and higher levels of awareness, guiding them to ever higher grades in the School.

The physical golden crown placed upon the heads of monarchs was merely a symbol of the halo or Crown of Wisdom glowing around the heads of the Wise. Unfortunately, men without Wisdom coveted the trappings of power associated with the divine right to rule. They conspired to usurp power from the Wise and, in culture after culture, men without Wisdom and without their Crown chakras open placed the physical golden crowns upon their heads. Thus began human civilization's downward spiral into darkness, resulting in our present dire circumstances.

The problem is that, without having the inner vision open and bringing the ability to see the Golden halo, the average person has no means of differentiating the Wise leaders from the pretenders. This situation can be likened to a preschool child having to choose between two teachers. One teacher tells the child that 2+2=4. The other teacher says that 2+2=5, but offers the child a candy cane to accept it. Lacking emotional maturity and a means of discernment, children will generally choose the candy cane and follow the false teachings of the false teacher. With modern media outlets working at the behest of false leaders, the candy canes are much larger and the omnipresent false message overwhelms the truth.

This is why the term 'saint' is so often accompanied by the phrase 'and a martyr.' Throughout history, false leaders have been more than willing to imprison, torture and murder those Wise teachers who threaten to disrupt the false power structure.

The irony is that the false leaders often manage to twist the words of Wise teachers and use them to advance their false agendas. Most religions are but a shadow of their original teachings and many directly contradict the intentions of their founders. Religion has become a tool used by the false leaders to control the masses.

With a clean, healthy diet for all, with the healing of environmental pollution and with regular practice of targeted meditation, the inner vision can be turned on more easily than you might expect.

When that occurs for the masses, Wise leaders can be identified and a Sophiacracy can commence. Until then, we must reform the way our leaders are chosen, finding the best means to select the most qualified candidates while eliminating corruption.

FINANCIAL REFORM

Money is the greatest corrupting influence in politics. The system is set up so that candidates need vast amounts of money to get elected. Only the wealthiest businesses and individuals can afford to make donations of a size that have an effect on candidates' chances. Hence, the candidates are beholden to those who make large donations. In exchange for being placed in power, politicians are willing to grant favors to and be influenced by these wealthy contributors. Thus, the nation has become a plutocracy, rule of the wealthy, in the guise of a democracy.

In the 2008 election, the Obama campaign spent over $760 Million. It stands to reason that the 2012 election will require even more money. That means that in his four years in office, President Obama has to average around $17 Million in donations each month in order to get reelected. Any opponent making a serious bid at challenging him must raise a similar amount of money.

The first thing that comes to mind is the waste. In a world where people are starving to death and lacking basic medical care, over $1.5 Billion will be spent on influence peddling in the 2012 Presidential election alone, not counting the hundreds of millions to be spent on gubernatorial, senatorial, and congressional elections. How much wellness care, food, education and infrastructure can be provided with $1.5 Billion?

With the need to amass $17 Million each month, how much time and energy is diverted from that needed to rule wisely? How much undue influence is exerted in exchange for those campaign contributions? The same holds true for Senators, Members of Congress and virtually every state and federal elected position.

The people don't count in elections anymore, except as pawns to be manipulated. To influence the masses, billions are spent on mass media. Television ads and news coverage decide who is elected.

Choice is based on 30 and 60 second emotional appeals via TV and radio commercials, and on sound bites on 'news' programs. Since the media outlets are owned by the plutocrats, the money spent on campaign contributions comes back to them in the end.

The plutocrats have now managed to corrupt and gain power over the Supreme Court. Recently, that body ruled that corporations are people and money is free speech. Hence it is now legal for corporations to spend unlimited amounts of money to influence elections. The corruption has become so blatant that even the pretense that citizens have power in this society is gone.

I challenge you to find 'free speech' in any definition of money in any economic text published prior to this ruling. As far as corporations being people, Merriam-Webster defines 'person' as: 'human, individual.' There is nothing about corporations or free speech in any common historical usage of these terms. These new definitions are cut from whole cloth by the corrupt minds of those who benefit from using money to influence politics.

Amazingly enough, the Supreme Court has ruled that a student holding up a poster that reads "Bong Hits for Jesus" is not protected under free speech, but corporations spending unlimited quantities to control elections are. Sadly, the Supreme Court, a body of unelected judges intended to be the last bastion, the final line of defense for the Constitution and the people, is now in the pockets of the plutocrats.

From the perspective of the plutocrats, political influence is an outstanding bargain. For a collective investment of a billion or so per campaign season, they reap trillions of dollars annually, directly and indirectly. Directly, they receive subsidies, grants and corporate welfare on a scale that dwarfs that spent on public welfare.

Indirect benefits are where the real profit lies, though. For instance, take the energy industry. Understanding the existence and potential of free energy, we know that the entire multi-trillion dollar energy industry is a farce. It exists only because of direct government intervention. For a few hundred million invested in campaigns and lobbies, the plutocrats pocket trillions of dollars while poisoning the planet and the people and bleeding our wealth.

144

Thanks to comparatively small investments in political contributions, the agribusiness, pharmaceutical, defense and other industries receive great benefit from government protectionism and favoritism. As should be expected, private bankers receive the best return on their investment.

From the fractionally tiny amount spent on political contributions, laws are enacted giving private bankers absolute control of the entire money supply. In an ironic twist of fate, the bankers can print the money that they use to influence the politicians to allow them to print the money. It would be comic if it weren't so tragic.

The most important factor in reforming politics and returning power to the people is removing the undue influence of money. Thankfully, in the age of the internet, this can easily be done. Substantive expression and debate of policy can take place without the need for vast sums of money.

Candidates and, more importantly, the voters, both deserve a level playing field. Citizens deserve to have elections decided through clear, objective appraisal of the candidates rather than by mass emotional imprinting and fear mongering. The following reforms will level the financial field:

1. Keep political finances in the realm of individual humans. That means campaign donations from individual citizens only. No more money from corporations, labor unions, banks, other businesses, clubs or any other organizations. If a particular organization is in favor of a particular candidate, the members of that organization can donate individually to that campaign. The organization itself may not.

2. Set limits on the amount each citizen can donate to each candidate per campaign. $250.00 per person per candidate seems like a fair number. With the prosperity of a Golden Society, virtually every citizen will be able to afford that amount should they choose to donate. Until then, this amount does not give an undue advantage to those who can afford it.

3. Set limits on the amount of money each candidate can collect and spend per campaign. For a Presidential election, say the

amount is $10 Million. That means that no candidate can collect or spend more than $10 Million on the campaign. When the collection limit is reached, the candidate must close down collection of donations. If the collection limit is not reached, the candidate may make up the difference out of personal funds, but may not spend over the limit. This equitable limitation of donations will level the playing field. Candidates will have to rely on substance rather than on hundreds of millions of dollars in mass marketing.

Spending and collection limits will compensate for even the small advantage that $250 contributors have over those with less money. Since most candidates will reach the contribution and spending limit in short order, there will not be much advantage gained from receiving donations from the higher end of the scale. The federal government will set the spending limits for Senate and Congress. State governments will be responsible to set the limits for state offices as will local governments for local elections.

4. Eliminate all PAC's (Political Action Committees), Super PAC's and all other forms of 'soft money.' These are nothing more than sophistry to circumvent election law and allow huge donations to influence politics. There supposedly is no coordination between candidates and PAC's, but in most cases the PAC's are operated by family members, business associates or political cronies of the candidates. Kudos to Stephen Colbert and Jon Stewart for satirizing this corrupt practice so poignantly.

POLITICAL PARTIES

If you look at donations by party, you will see that the same banks, corporations and industries donate to both parties in roughly equal amounts. Pharmaceuticals, banking, defense contractors, agribusiness and the energy industry are perennially the top contributors to both parties. Donating to both parties means the donors don't need to be concerned about which party holds power. Each party is beholden to the same donors who ultimately wield the real power. In the end, there is only one political party in the U.S., the Republocrats.

Anyone still rooting for either party is demonstrating how deeply duped they are. I'm not saying this to denigrate or insult these people. Billions of dollars are spent on mass media to generate and maintain the illusion of democracy. Small wonder so many fall prey to it.

The political parties exist only to continue the illusion of democracy and citizen participation while distracting the people from what is really going on behind the scenes. The current political system is analagous to a sports league in which every team is owned by the same organization. The owners wouldn't care which team you rooted for as long as you rooted for one, gave your allegiance to it and spent your money on it. The media wouldn't care either as long as they made money broadcasting the games and reporting on the teams.

To further the sports analogy, look at any campaign rally. The only differences between political rallies and high school pep rallies are the money spent, the media coverage and the age of the participants. Political rallies are orchestrated psychological ploys designed to increase emotional investment and enthusiasm. No real discussion or substance takes place.

When looked at objectively, the two party system makes absolutely no sense as a form of representative government. Each party creates a platform, taking a specific stand on each issue. Basically, what is being said is that out of 350 million people, there are only two perspectives, two ways of seeing things and two ways of doing things. Ridiculous! In reality, there should be 350 million political parties, because each individual is unique and has his or her own unique perspective regardless of how similar it may be to that of others.

The two party system is merely the 'Divide and Conquer' ethos distilled to its most basic essence. The more people can be motivated to fight each other, the less likely they will be to look for the real culprits or focus on real solutions.

I am quite certain the Founding Fathers did not intend a party system since political parties are not part of the Constitution and none existed for some years after its signing. Reform of the political party system will end its undue and corrupting influence.

Ban all political parties. It's that simple. Citizens of a Golden Society have no need to band together to take and hold power. By banning parties and decentralizing the political process, the creativity of the people will be unleashed. As individual citizens gain more influence in politics, there will be space for new ideas and unorthodox solutions. Ideas will have to stand on their own merit without party propaganda to bolster them. If a proposal has merit, it will be seriously considered. Elected officials can make decisions based on merit rather than on party loyalty.

If I were to join a political party, I would want it to be the "No More Parties Party!" A political party that counts among its prime purposes the end of all political parties would not only be a powerful force for change, it would pique my penchant for paradox and irony.

CAMPAIGN PROCEDURE REFORM

Currently, campaigns are expensive, drawn out affairs with little substance and much flash. They are a strange combination of circus and endurance contest. By reforming campaign procedures, we can add substance, level the playing field, reduce costs and make candidates more accessible to all. The information age provides our solution.

The internet can be the great leveler in campaign procedure. Combined with other media and information technology, it can provide an equal forum for all candidates.

A general election website can provide general information on all candidates broken down by region and political race and include links to candidates' individual websites. It can also be used to compare and contrast candidates' positions.

On their individual websites, candidates can use their creativity to express their messages and convey their policies. With advances in digital video recording, editing and computer graphics, campaigns can economically create videos expressing their standpoints in great detail. Candidates can interact with the public through online chat sessions, question and answer periods, blogs and video chats. Through internet technology, we can move beyond the flash and drama into a realm of substantive communication and productive debate. The leadership can connect directly with the people.

Campaign commercials should become a thing of the past. The election commission would be wise to run public service announcements informing and reminding the public of an upcoming election and encouraging them to visit the general election website for information on the races and candidates. Other than that, there should be no campaign advertisements. People have the right to choose their leaders objectively without being bombarded with emotional imprinting.

The candidates can use their creativity to interact with the public in other ways. Town hall meetings, community meals, speeches, days at the amusement park and even more ways we haven't considered yet can be used to meet with the public.

Personally, I would like to see a candidate convoy and mobile political fair. At least for part of the campaign season, it would be productive for candidates to travel as a group from town to town, setting up an exposition in which each can interact with the public directly and take turns speaking formally.

Remember, only the Presidential election is nationwide. The remainder are confined to individual states or districts, so the logistics of such a proposition are very feasible. This type of traveling political fair would be economical for the campaigns, facilitate the process for the public, and, hopefully, bring civility to elections.

The media can remain involved by interviewing candidates, conducting debates and airing public service announcements reminding citizens of upcoming elections and encouraging them to vote. They can also run fact checks, investigate corruption and research candidates' backgrounds.

TERM LIMITS

Term limits are another means of ridding the system of corruption and restoring political power to the citizenry. Career politicians tend to end up insulated from the public, have to focus much of their time seeking contributions for reelection, and, rather than voting their consciences and the will of their constituents, often vote with an eye to their next campaign. Term limits will eliminate these issues.

- Limit all elected officials to one consecutive term in office.
- Institute a 10 year waiting period between holding elected offices or between accepting a government job after holding office or holding office after having a government job.

It is that simple. By limiting politicians to one term, there will be no concerns over reelection or campaign financing. Elected officials will be free to focus on the job at hand.

Even with term limits, there are those who would make a career of politics by holding government staff positions between holding elected offices. Less scrupulous politicians could use their influence while in office to give jobs to cronies. Then, when the cronies are elected, they could return the favor. By instating a 10 year waiting period before an elected official can take a government job and before an ex-government employee can be elected to office, favoritism, nepotism and career politics can be eliminated.

There are over 350 million U.S. citizens. There are only 537 federal elected offices: 100 Senators, 435 Representatives, one President and one Vice President. At that ratio, there will still be plenty of qualified candidates after term limits are enacted.

If an honest, concerned citizen is elected to Congress, then ten years after leaving office he or she can run for Senate or President. The intervening time will have to be spent working in the private sector. Term limits applied in this way will keep politicians in touch with the public and ensure the type of citizen led government that the Founding Fathers intended.

When term limits are instituted, it may be wise to extend the term of a Congressperson to 3 years. One-third will be seniors, one-third will be sophomores and one-third will be freshmen. This breakdown will ensure a pool of veterans to assist the newcomers since there no longer will be any incumbent Congresspersons to act as mentors.

LOBBY REFORM

When the Constitution was written, the Founding Fathers intended for citizens to be empowered to petition their elected representatives. Since there were no high speed transportation or mass communication systems, they devised a means, called lobbying, for citizens to invest others to represent their interests. In modern times, this lobby system has been used as a loophole for the plutocrats to use vast sums of money to corrupt the system.

Hundreds of millions are spent on professional lobbyists to influence government officials. Often these lobbyists are ex-elected officials or ex-political staffers who have left their government posts to grow wealthy using their insider connections to influence politics. Professional lobbying is often accompanied by sizable campaign donations, giving lobbyists far more influence than the average citizen.

The system was originally designed to make it easier for the average citizen to petition their government. Instead, it has become exactly the opposite. Lobbying has become a tool of the plutocrats. Average citizens are shunted aside since they lack the resources to influence political campaigns.

Now that we have the internet, wireless communication and high speed transportation, the need for lobbyists is obsolete. People can send emails or make calls directly to the offices of elected officials. If the need is sufficiently urgent, they can board airplanes or take road trips to petition their representatives in person. Since elected officials maintain offices in their home territories, it is also possible to petition them directly without ever leaving their home district.

- End all professional lobbying.
- Limit lobbying to individual citizens only, no businesses or organizations.

It is that simple. Ending professional lobbying will get the money out of petitioning the government and end that form of influence peddling. Lobbying by businesses and organizations is not necessary and is unfair to private citizens. If a business or organization wants to petition the government, the owners or individual members can do so as individual citizens. "Hi, my name is so and so. I own a business in your district and the following policy affects my business in the following ways."

Our government was intended to be by the people, of the people and for the people. Notice that corporations, banks, unions and other organizations are not mentioned. We are individual citizens first, and members of other organizations second. If petitioning the government is limited to individual citizens, then it will be equal and fair for all.

ELECTION REFORM

Electoral College vs Popular Vote: The electoral college is an outdated, cumbersome and unnecessary process. Like lobbying, it was intended for a different technological era. When ·electors had to travel for days or weeks on horseback or carriage to cast the votes of their constituents, the electoral college made sense. With modern communication and transportation technology, it is time to change.

Replace the electoral college with a straight popular vote. This change will bring a new level of fairness to the electoral process. Due to the anachronistic electoral college, politicians currently focus on the states with the largest numbers of electoral votes. They also tend to ignore the states in which they know they don't have a chance of winning. It doesn't make strategic sense for them to spend money on or commit energy to a state they know they will lose. With the electoral college system, even if a candidate earns 40% of the popular vote, in many states they would get no electoral votes.

Citizens in uncontested states end up being unable to connect with candidates. A percentage of constituents are ignored since they hold no political capital to help with a candidate's election bid. This situation creates voter apathy. There is no motivation to vote knowing their vote won't count.

The worst effect of the whole process is there have been candidates who have won the popular vote, but actually lost the election. It is time to end the electoral college and replace it with the popular vote.

Candidate Selection: With political parties discontinued, there will be a need for a new form of candidate selection. Certain criteria will have to be met, such as gathering a specific number of signatures. The number should be high enough to establish that a candidate is serious, but low enough to keep candidacy from being exclusive.

Without the two party system, there will be many more candidates than before. This will necessitate run-off elections. An election will be won when a candidate garners a majority of the popular vote. Instead of party based primaries, there will be preliminary and run-off elections.

If no candidate wins a majority in the preliminary election, lower placing candidates will be eliminated based on a mathematical formula. Run-offs will continue, mathematically eliminating lower placed candidates until one candidate attains a majority. With high tech election procedures and a well informed citizenry, minimal time will be needed between run-offs, even a little as one week.

Election Devices: I find it fascinating that with SSL encryption, we can safely bank and conduct business online, but we have not integrated online voting into our society. Imagine an online voting system. Citizens could log in with a voter number or username and password and vote from the comfort of their own home or from their smart phone or laptop.

Also, consider the idea of a larger voting window. Currently, polling stations are only open for around 12 to 14 hours. There are often long lines and it can take hours to vote. Many people don't have the time available during such a small window.

Imagine if voting lasted several days. During that time, anyone could go to a polling station or log in to vote from anywhere at anytime. Exit polls would not be allowed to publish their results until after all polling is closed so that preliminary results don't affect later voting. With online voting, results can be tallied accurately and almost instantly upon poll closing.

If it hasn't been achieved yet, it is only a matter of time before internet security has reached a point that we can make such a transition. Evidence suggests that it would be more secure and accurate than Diebold voting machines. These are so easily defrauded that our current elections do not meet U.N. standards and would not be certified. It is highly ironic that the founder and bastion of modern democracy has unverifiable and un-certifiable elections.

Until such time as we can transition to secure online voting, at the very least, Diebold machines and punch ballots should be replaced with the scan type voting machines. With punch ballots, there is the risk of the dreaded hanging chad. The programming of Diebold machines is questionable and there is no printout or other verifiable physical record.

If Diebold machines could be modified to give a printout that can be verified by the voter before being deposited into a secure box, there would at least be some measure of accountability. Yet, they are still prone to fraud.

Just as with the multiple choice tests from grade school, coloring in the appropriate bubbles on a scan sheet using a number two pencil has been demonstrated to be the best combination of accuracy and speed in vote tallying. These machines can count thousands of votes in a matter of minutes. If there are discrepancies, the hard copies that can be counted by hand to verify the results.

With political reforms restoring power to the citizens, voter apathy will decline and participation will increase. With the transition to simple, easy voting methods, larger voting windows, and an end to political corruption, I believe participation will approach 100%.

BEWARE OF REPERCUSSIONS

Political reforms that remove the money from politics and restore the power of government to the people will seriously erode the control of the plutocrats. With so much at stake, they are not likely to let go quietly. They have used all manner of unscrupulous means in their bid for power, including starting wars, poisoning populations and creating false flag attacks. Don't expect them to wash their hands and walk away peacefully.

I was proud of the Occupy Movement and the nonviolent way they went about their protests. I wasn't surprised to see it repressed with violence. Even with images of pump bottles of pepper spray being dosed on peaceful demonstrators and footage of riot police firing tear gas and using their batons, the press often managed to spin the story as violence instigated by the protestors. Remember that the press is in the pocket of the plutocrats even more so now than during the Sixties.

If political reform is passed, the remainder of the Golden reforms can be put in place more easily. Everyone, including the plutocrats, will be happier and more fulfilled in a Golden Society. They just are not aware and do not appreciate that yet.

From their perspective, the plutocrats stand to lose all the power they conspired and connived for so long to acquire. When they see it slipping away, they may pull out all the stops. Hopefully, our soldiers and police will hesitate if ordered to fire on their own people.

It is of extreme importance that the movement for change be peaceful and nonviolent. The concepts presented here are already going to push the programmed minds of many to their limits of acceptance. Even though average citizens are well aware of the dysfunction of the current system and of the great need for change, any association with violence may push them in the wrong direction. Conversely, if violence is used by the ruling powers against the agents of change, sympathy will be engendered in the general public, inspiring many to join the cause.

Self-defense is everyone's right, but violence should not be initiated as a means of social change. The transition to a Golden Society can, and hopefully will, be accomplished peacefully. Focus your thoughts on a peaceful outcome, but be prepared just in case. It will take an iron will to bring about the changes we crave. Focus on the goal. It will be worth it.

All of the technologies written about so far in this book exist right now. Free energy technology has existed since the early 1900s in the time of Tesla. Large scale pumping and hydraulic technologies are used everyday in the oil and mining industries as well as in populated areas that lie below sea level such as Holland and New Orleans.

Desalinization technology exists and is in use today in many nations. Offshore oil platforms are currently in wide use. Creating offshore desalinization plants would only be a matter of combining these existing technologies.

Organic farming and animal husbandry technologies already exist. To become universal, their use need only be encouraged. Living machines and other naturally based, nonpolluting forms of waste reclamation exist today. Many preventative measures and cures for cancer and other debilitating diseases are already available. To bring them into common use, we need only supersede profit as the dominant motive in the medical industry.

Humanity already has everything it needs to create every change proposed so far. We only need the will to manifest the vision.

This chapter is devoted to promising technologies that are on the horizon, some of which already have working prototypes. The possibilities and potentials presented by these technologies provide even greater cause for optimism.

ANTI-GRAVITY

Anti-gravity technology already exists in prototypical stages. I have seen videos of private inventors able to achieve the effect on a small scale. I have also seen video footage from as early as the middle of the 20th century showing the U.S. Air Force having success as well. The limiting factor was the amount of energy needed. Their prototype vehicle was tethered to a large power cable. Though the vehicle's range was limited by this cable, controlled anti-gravity flight was achieved.

With free energy devices, the power limitation is solved. Practical anti-gravity technology can be a reality in our lifetimes. It only needs to be wrested from the hands of the energy-military complex.

Imagine a society where anti-gravity technology is in common use. Roads would become obsolete along with the expense of road construction and maintenance. Personal vehicles could carry passengers to any location with ease. Rush hour traffic and road rage will become historical anomalies. With automated GPS integration, long journeys can become relaxing, enjoyable experiences.

With anti-gravity and free energy, the world is literally at everyone's fingertips for the cost of a vehicle. A family can watch the wildebeest migration in Africa or the polar bears in Canada from the comfort of their vehicle. They can go shopping in Paris or dine in Shanghai for no more cost than going to the corner market.

Cargo can be loaded into huge vessels and shipped across continents and oceans for pennies. Unmanned smaller anti-gravity containers can also be used for cargo. With current GPS and computer technology, goods can be sent directly to specific destinations without need for pilots or crew.

Disaster relief can be delivered directly to victims. Floating anti-gravity hospitals can be set up on site. Anti-gravity clinics can bring traveling medical services to remote villages and towns.

Anti-gravity recreational vehicles and truly mobile homes can be created. Many people will choose a life of movement and will bring their homes with them. With this freedom of movement, borders will become meaningless. If it isn't already in place, a one world nation would have to develop along with anti-gravity technology.

Anti-gravity would also expedite the exploration of space. As the technology advances, the vastness of our galaxy and universe will open to us. This one invention, when coupled with existing technologies, will create massive changes in our culture and quality of life. Perhaps, this is why it is still under lock and key.

NANOTECHNOLOGY

Nanotechnology definitely exists in the prototypical stages and possibly in the operational stage. Nanotechnology is technology that operates within dimensions and tolerances of less than 100 nanometers. A nanometer is one billionth of a meter, so the scale is extremely minute.

Nanites are tiny robots that manipulate individual atoms and molecules. In the 1990s, I saw on an educational TV channel an electron microscope video of very basic working nanites. If this information was being made available to the public then, I can only imagine how much more developed the technology is in classified military laboratories today.

With over a decade of continued research and development along with the consistent doubling of computer capacity, I am confident there is functional nanotechnology in existence today. It is kept secret because the military applications can be devastating. Conversely, imagine the beneficial applications made possible by the ability to manipulate matter on molecular and atomic levels.

One of the most exciting potentials is the capacity to clean up the entire waste stream, removing all past, present and future pollutants from the environment. Nanites can break down molecules into their component elements. Imagine the potential for the disposal of toxic waste. Dangerous chemical compounds can be broken down into harmless constituents: hydrogen, oxygen, carbon, iron, phosphorous, etc. Better yet, these constituents can be recombined into useful products.

Even as we clean our landfills and toxic waste dumps, we will gain raw materials for future production. With the reuse of everything that has been discarded or is currently in use, we should never need to extract raw materials again. We can save money and resources, eliminate pollution and rehabilitate the natural environment through the conscious integration of this technology.

You can think of the application of nanotechnology as a mechanized version of the replicators in *Star Trek*. Waste is broken down and stored. When an item is desired, its molecular structure is programmed into a computer. The nanites then use raw materials to construct the item based on the computer template.

The medical implications are equally exciting. Nanites are small enough to be injected into the body and can even enter individual cells to conduct repairs. The day is not far off when programmed nanites can be injected into cancer patients. The nanites will seek out and destroy all cancerous cells. One of the most deadly diseases can be cured in a matter of hours or days with no harmful side effects.

The same is true for heart disease and other ailments. Plaque can be removed from arteries. Bones can be knit. Internal damage can be repaired. The possibilities go beyond what my mind can imagine. Not only can major diseases be eliminated, but wellness care costs will plummet. Is this why we haven't heard more about this technology?

DIMENSIONAL PORTALS

Another potential technology whose possibilities fascinate me is that of dimensional portals. I have read theoretical documents concerning this technology and have heard stories of clandestine experiments, but I have seen no hard evidence that it exists yet. Nevertheless, with the advances in quantum physics, it is only a matter of time.

Imagine opening a portal, stepping through and instantly ending up in Times Square, Bangkok, Buenos Aires or any other place you choose. This ability would decentralize society and create a movement back to rural life. Homes could be sited in the most remote locations without disturbing the natural surroundings. All of the amenities of modern society would be available only a few steps away.

Many people will still choose to live in urban environments and smaller communities for the sense of togetherness and social fellowship. Yet, they will still benefit from this technology as they also will be able to travel with ease.

Dimensional portals can potentially revolutionize space travel. Imagine opening a portal and stepping through onto another planet on the other side of the galaxy. As we come to understand quantum physics and fractal geometry, we will realize that the universe is much more accessible than previously thought. As we become a space faring people, the possibilities will be endless.

3-D PRINTERS

3-D printers do in three dimensions what standard printers do in two. A two dimensional printer takes a preprogrammed image and prints it on a sheet of paper. A 3-D printer takes a preprogrammed three dimensional image and constructs it in three dimensions. These devices already exist on a small scale. Soon they will exist on larger scales as well.

Imagine being able to program the image of a building into a large scale 3-D printer. Then, you can just stand back and watch as it automatically builds the building. The construction and manufacturing industries will be revolutionized.

Another exciting feature is that these devices are self-replicating. If you buy one 3-D printer, you can use it to construct others. You will only need the construction medium and computer programs to fabricate anything that you choose.

INTEGRATING TECHNOLOGY IN A GOLDEN SOCIETY

There is no way to arrest progress. As we move into the future, many possibilities will be presented by new technologies. As with everything, these technologies can be used positively or negatively. Their potential dangers may cause fear for some individuals.

The issue, however, is not with the technologies themselves, but with how we choose to use them. As Shakespeare wrote, *"Nothing is good or bad, but thinking makes it so."* A spoon can be used to kill someone or to feed and nourish them. The choice is with the user and blame or praise cannot be placed on the spoon.

The only way to ensure the positive use of new technologies is to transition to a Golden Society. Only by living from the heart will the choice always be made to use all technology, old and new, in positive, constructive ways. Creating a Golden Society is the means to save humanity from self-destruction.

CHAPTER 18
THE CELESTIAL NEIGHBORHOOD

"Beware the bearers of false gifts and their broken promises
Much pain but still time
Believe
There is good out there
We oppose the deceivers
The conduit is closing"

WRITTEN IN ASCII COMPUTER LANGUAGE IN A CROP CIRCLE
TRANSLATION FROM THE DOCUMENTARY FILM
MAYAN PROPHECIES AND CROP CIRCLES

A society that is based on the realities of Life must consciously understand its place in the larger scheme. The reality is that the Universe is filled with life, more life in greater variety than can be imagined. Science fiction cannot approach describing everything that is out there, though some hits close to the mark in certain cases.

Despite the massive propaganda campaign dedicated to influencing us otherwise, polls show that well over half of the population now believes in extraterrestrial life. That number has climbed steadily over the years as incontrovertible evidence mounts. Dr. Stephen Greer and the Disclosure Project along with other organizations classifying themselves under the umbrella of Exopolitics have done an excellent job of presenting facts using clear scientific means. The Disclosure Project gathered hundreds of military, intelligence, government and corporate officials and gave them a forum to disclose en masse their first hand accounts relating to the truth of extraterrestrial activity.

With the spread of digital video and information technology, there is more video and photographic proof uploaded to the internet every day. From backyard amateur video to gun camera footage from air forces around the globe, the evidence mounts despite the best efforts of those who would control this information as a means of controlling the population. Some of the best footage comes from NASA cameras on space shuttle and earlier missions. This reality can no longer be dismissed as quacks seeing swamp gas.

Even without this hard evidence, an objective examination of reality would convince most people. The Milky Way Galaxy alone has 100 Billion stars. There are an estimated 350 Billion galaxies in the universe. Our universe is one of billions in the Cosmos. With this perspective of the overwhelming size of Creation, does anyone really believe that humans are the only intelligent life?

Understanding the size and scope of Creation, can anyone really believe the story that so many religions sell? Did a deity create the entire cosmos over the course of trillions upon trillions of years solely to create a proving ground for humans? Is the purpose of Creation really a celestial trial so that we can live for around 60 years to be judged on our 'goodness' and sent for eternity to Heaven or Hell? Does this deity really have nothing better to do? Can he not think of any better uses for all of that vastness? Does the being that created all of that sublime magnificence really have such low self-esteem that our 'salvation' depends on spending most of our time praising him and telling him how great he is? It just doesn't make sense.

There is indeed an Intelligence behind Creation that some would label as a Deity. Every part of that Creation is alive and has awareness. Humans are just a small, yet equally important part of the Whole. Everything in Creation has a purpose. Each form of life is on its own path of growth, expansion and learning. Everything that has a magnetic field is alive and aware on some level, from rocks to stars. Stars and galaxies are immense forms of life and have learning progressions that are far beyond human comprehension. The Creator certainly doesn't need us to tell Him (or Her) how great He is in order for Creation to function properly.

Quantum physics and fractal geometry are proving scientifically what mystics have been telling us for millennia. We live in a multidimensional universe. In addition to extraterrestrial beings, there are extra-dimensional beings as well. There are higher and lower dimensional levels and each is teeming with its corresponding life forms. Spiritual and mystical natured people have been aware of this for eons. Through specific meditations, these mystics have been able to activate dormant parts of the brain that are used to sense and experience these other levels of Creation.

The interpretations of these experiences differ based on training, background and predilection. One person's lower dimensional alien life form is another person's demon or devil. One person's higher dimensional life form is another person's angel or god. The nature of the life form doesn't change, only the interpretation.

Virtually every human has the capacity to activate these higher brain functions and to experience directly the multidimensional nature of Life. Anyone who sees through to the Divine fabric of Creation finds themselves free of temporal authority and domination. For this reason, fallen religions have ruthlessly obliterated anything outside their dogma, labeling it witchcraft, devil worship and sin. For the same reason, plutocratic governments have instituted environmental pollution, poor diet and ineffective education. By dumbing down the population, dampening sensitivity and eliminating spiritual empowerment and independence, the masses can be kept tractable and subservient.

To achieve our potential as a fully functional, heart-based Golden Society and to consciously take our part in the School of Life, we must come to know and understand our celestial neighbors. As with everything on the polarity levels of Creation, there are positive and negative extraterrestrial and extra-dimensional beings. We must understand that each of them are on their own individual and collective learning progressions in the School of Life.

They are no more or less important than we are. They are simply in different grades in the same School. There has already been clandestine contact with some of these beings. Eventually, there will be overt direct contact and the general population will have to deal with the understanding that they exist. We must get to know them and objectively decide how to interact.

POSITIVE BEINGS

Undoubtedly, there are positive beings with more highly evolved cultures than our own. As such, they will have a greater understanding of the purpose of Life and our place in the School of Life. It stands to reason that these beings would have an ethos of non-interference, much like the Prime Directive in *Star Trek*. They would be unwilling to intrude on our learning progression without invitation.

As we evolve to a heart-based Golden Society, our readiness to interact with our positive celestial neighbors will be demonstrated. When they make contact with a benevolent human government or with benevolent representatives of humanity, we can invite these beings to interact more extensively with all humans.

Cultural, educational and technological exchange programs can be established. Imagine the advances in energy, medicine, space travel, spiritual understanding and so much more that will be available through contact with positive extraterrestrial cultures. Imagine the perspective we will gain on our own history by interacting with a culture that has been observing us for thousands of years. It will happen. It is only a matter of time and of our willingness.

Our current governments are corrupt or under the influence of the corrupt, and, therefore, have abdicated the authority to represent free and conscious humans. Until the time comes that a standing terrestrial government embraces the principles of a Golden Society and thus legitimizes its authority, free individuals must be willing to serve as the representatives of the free peoples of Earth to any positive extraterrestrial and extra-dimensional peoples that wish to interact with humanity. It is time for the process to begin. The majority of humans are ready.

On behalf of all free peoples of Earth, I hereby invite positive extraterrestrial and extra-dimensional societies to make contact to begin the process of overt, conscious and intentional interspecies interaction and exchange.

166

NEGATIVE BEINGS

We would be remiss if we didn't acknowledge the existence of negative beings as well as positive. In the School of Life, there are beings other than humans who also have yet to learn that it is wrong to violate the sovereignty of other individuals and other civilizations. From these beings, we must protect ourselves and, hopefully, show and teach them a better way.

There are those who claim that negative aliens have been manipulating human culture for centuries or millennia. While I cannot prove or disprove that claim, as someone who lives from a place of openness to all possibilities, I have to acknowledge the possibility. Creation is vast and there are many life forms out there. Humanity is relatively young and primitive. It wouldn't take a great deal of effort for a more technologically advanced culture to take advantage of our ignorance and naiveté.

Regardless of the accuracy of that claim, a Golden Society is the answer. Heart chakra beings cannot be so manipulated. The act of coming together to create a Golden Society will negate and successfully counter efforts at control by manipulative beings, whether human or alien. A free society cannot be controlled. It can only be destroyed by force. Better that than to live as slaves.

OUR CELESTIAL NEIGHBORHOOD

As part of waking up and becoming a conscious society, we must acknowledge and make an objective effort to get to know our celestial neighbors. This is a fascinating and exciting time to be a human. Our future promises great adventure! I look forward to it eagerly.

CHAPTER 19
WHAT CAN I DO?

"No matter how exotic human civilization becomes, no matter the developments of life and society nor the complexity of the machine/human interface, there always come interludes of lonely power when the course of humankind depends upon the relatively simple actions of single individuals."

FROM *DUNE MESSIAH*, BY FRANK HERBERT

The sheer number of humanitarian, environmental and other charity organizations in the world today demonstrates the collective human desire and willingness to strive for positive change. The Occupy Movement showed the widespread nature of public discontent. The desire for and movement toward change is clear. A cohesive, coherent plan and organized effort is all that is lacking. Now, we have a blueprint.

When someone asks me what they can do to make the world a better place, I answer in metaphor, **'When one light bulb grows brighter, the entire room gets brighter'**

Become a better person. Grow, learn, expand, attain fulfillment and self-actualization. Be happy. Live joy. As you become and embody your True Self, the Light will radiate ever more brightly from your being.

Doing so, you will have raised the collective vibration of the entire human race and the entire planet. Others will notice the brightness emanating from you. When they inquire about your joyful state, there will be an open window through which you can inspire and guide them.

COLLECTIVE ACTION

While we will soon discuss at length means of embodying your True Self and brightening your inner Light, there are also collective actions that can be taken.

Political Movement: The grass roots Occupy Movement demonstrated the growing discontent with the current economic and political state. While I celebrate the spirit behind the movement, it lacked direction and a specific plan. While the protesters know a better life is possible, they don't know yet how to get there. It is difficult to articulate heart chakra consciousness in political and economic terms. This is untrodden ground for modern human civilization.

This blueprint provides the plan. The collective focus and will of the people must provide the means to achieve it. If the energy of the discontented masses is focused together on a specific plan, phenomenal changes will occur.

Thanks to popular modern works such as *What the Bleep?* and *The Secret*, ancient understandings of the effects of consciousness on quantum reality are becoming common knowledge. With millions of people focused on creating a Golden Society, the Laws of Nature will ensure that it manifests. Protest movements have shown the will. The *Blueprint* gives direction. With will, direction and focus, manifestation is assured.

A political movement is required here, not necessarily a new political party. The two party system has a virtual stranglehold on the political process in the U.S. Rather than fighting upstream by trying to create and validate a new political party, it makes more sense to use the existing infrastructure. Substance is more important than labels. Advocates of a Golden Society can join either political party, running on a platform of Golden reform.

This is not unlike the Tea Party movement within the Republican Party. Rather than fighting against the current structure, it can be used to our advantage. Golden Society candidates can run in either wing of the two party system or as Independents. Support those candidates. When enough have been elected, power will return to the people and reforms can be enacted.

170

Only about half of eligible U.S. voters participate in elections. The remainder have become too apathetic to participate in what they know to be an unjust system. If the disenfranchised majority become energized by a true plan for the future, a Golden wave of reform can be initiated.

Studies show that already over 25% of the population believes in many of the principles espoused in this book. That is a higher percentage than votes for the winning candidates in Presidential elections. If that 25% fully mobilizes, political power will return to the people.

New voters are registering as Independents at a higher rate than those registering as Democrats or Republicans, further demonstrating dissatisfaction with the morass of modern political dysfunction. The average person no longer associates with either party. Disgruntlement abounds. Citizen discontent is at an all time high.

By banding together and rallying behind a common cause, the disaffected masses can initiate sweeping reform. Every member of the House of Representatives is up for reelection every two years. One out of every three Senate seats is also up for reelection every two years. Within two years, the entire House and one-third of the Senate can be replaced. That is more than enough to begin actualizing our reforms.

Let us hope that these changes can be made peacefully through the electoral process prior to the final planned meltdown of the financial system and crash of the economy. With debilitating economic collapse will come violent protest and revolution. That is the inevitable consequence of widespread poverty, hunger and the destruction of personal wealth.

Hopefully, we can enact our vision prior to this taking place. If not, at least we have a plan to guide us out of the chaos into a Golden tomorrow.

<u>Spread the Word</u>: If you are inspired by this blueprint and moved to share it with others, take advantage of modern information technology. Use social media, write emails, send texts. Make it go viral.

Tell your friends and family, neighbors and coworkers. Introduce others to this book so they can see for themselves the comprehensive and cohesive nature of the plan. Share it with Love and be accepting of those who aren't yet ready to grasp the concepts. If you are motivated enough, run for office. You can help lead humanity to its Golden future, its divine inheritance.

Unleash Your Creativity: The website www.1earthpeople.com was created as a forum for interaction, exchange and promotion of a Golden Society. Share your ideas. I don't have a patent on truth or creativity. I have only created a canvas on which humanity can paint a Golden future, a framework over which others will construct a monument to freedom.

My great hope is that through a Golden Society, the creativity and potential of every human will be unleashed. Use your creativity, knowledge and expertise to generate ideas and solutions I have never considered and to refine ones that I have.

Just remember that the purpose of Life and of our society is the free growth and fulfillment of each individual. Base your ideas on these principles and all will be well.

Join the Nation: Since no standing government is committed to the principles of a Golden Society or to creating a civilization of the heart, let's start our own. We can begin a borderless nation of free peoples dedicated to the mutual support of those around the globe who are committed to manifesting these ideals.

It doesn't have to begin in the U.S. Free people anywhere can initiate change in their home countries. As the current dysfunctional system continues to collapse and ever more people become disillusioned, eventually the wave of momentum will sweep a Golden Society into office in some courageous, progressive country. The remainder will inevitably follow suit.

PERSONAL ACTION

Make Your Light Bulb Brighter: This next section is probably going to tick off some yogis, because I am going to share an ancient meditation technique that has been kept secret for thousands of years. There is a reason it has only been passed down orally through initiation. The technique is extremely potent and deeply transformational. Just as a loaded pistol in the hands of a toddler, it has the potential to do great damage to those who don't understand it.

Nevertheless, there is a method to my madness. I have chosen to share this information because the alternatives are most dire. Humanity is at a crossroads. If drastic positive changes do not occur in the very near future, one of two outcomes is almost certain. Either the general population will be directly enslaved by the plutocrats or the planet will be degraded to the extent that it can no longer support human life. Either consequence is worse than that of a few knuckleheads abusing the information I am about to share.

I am not going to teach the entire technique here, but I will share enough that if you apply it diligently and wisely, your life will transform positively and powerfully. This technique acts through the endocrine system, using the life force to stimulate psycho-emotional development and higher brain function. It will help erase the emotional and cultural programming imprinted since birth. It will also help bring to the surface any buried trauma that has been sabotaging your life. Knowing this, perhaps you can now understand the danger implicit in its wanton use.

When we suffer trauma that our being is not mature enough to handle, that trauma is stored in the network of psychic channels that surround and interpenetrate the physical body. There it remains, unconsciously influencing decisions and sabotaging behavior. Psychotherapy alone is a slow and comparatively ineffectual attempt to address this trauma. There is an adage, "You can't use the mind to heal the mind." Therapy works from the outside in and can take decades or an entire lifetime to achieve the breakthroughs that transform a life.

This meditation technique cultivates life force energy and moves it through the psychic channels, gently but powerfully bringing trauma and other emotional debris to the surface. Ideally, this process is taught to people who have already developed a certain level of emotional maturity and are ready to deal with the debris as it rises to awareness. It would be beneficial if you have a support system in place to help deal with these emotions as they arise.

This technique also activates the third ventricle of the brain. This is the seat of higher consciousness within the body and has been referred to metaphorically by many cultures with terms such as the Crystal Palace and the Cave of Brahma. In the third ventricle reside the pineal and pituitary glands and the hypothalamus.

By bringing life force energy to the third ventricle to stimulate these glands, this meditation technique, on a physiological level, activates higher consciousness. Eventually, after consistent practice, the pituitary will secrete a hormone which will connect with the pineal. There will also be an electrical, energetic connection.

This causes an incredible reaction within the brain. The corpus callosum activates, allowing both hemispheres of the brain to communicate and to be active simultaneously. Thousands of dormant neurons awaken, activating unused brain potential.

When you feel these individual dormant neurons fire, you will understand why some cultures call this experience 'Opening the Thousand Petaled Lotus.' The hypothalamus produces large quantities of endorphins, the pleasure hormones. This is why spiritual ecstasy accompanies the attainment of this level of enlightenment.

Even in the early stages of practicing this technique, stimulation of the pineal gland will help to attain a state of objective self-awareness, also known as causal awareness. It is important to be in this state as the buried trauma and debris rise to the surface.

Studies show that when a person mentally relives a trauma, the body's physiological responses are exactly the same as when the trauma was originally experienced. Simply remembering and reliving trauma is tantamount to self-torture. By bringing your awareness to a causal level, you can observe the experience with detachment and distance, the way an audience member observes a play.

From a detached, unemotional place, you can observe yourself as you recall the trauma. By witnessing the experience causally, you can not only observe the experience, but also how the experience affected you emotionally and how it has affected your life since. By objectively observing the experience from a detached, unemotional place, you can release the trauma once and for all, rather than reliving it repeatedly.

Existing in this causal place is like simultaneously being both an audience member and actor in a play. Attaining this level of awareness is one of the keys to living a directed, conscious life. It is rather simple, and with a bit of practice, anyone can do it.

Imagine rising out of your body and looking down at yourself. From there, you can observe yourself in your actions, or in this case, in your memories. If you still feel your emotions from this place, rise higher. In cases of extremely charged emotions, you may need to rise all the way into space, so you are looking down at the globe of the Earth and your tiny body sitting or standing on the surface. By finding a place beyond your emotions, you will be able to effectively observe and release the trauma.

It is good to have a confidant to discuss matters as they arise. In the case of extreme trauma, it may be good to have a mentor or even a therapist or other healing professional. The meditation technique will bring trauma and emotional debris to the surface. You must have the emotional maturity and the tools to deal with what rises and have the support you need to process it.

There are several dangers of practicing this technique about which you should be informed. The first is the potential of bringing to the surface buried traumas that you are not yet ready to confront. They were buried for a reason. If you haven't developed the emotional maturity to process them, you may traumatize yourself further.

On multiple occasions, I have seen repressed memories of childhood molestation surface into memory as the result of practicing this technique. Be certain you have the maturity, balance and determination to deal with whatever arises. Have a support system available should it be needed.

The next danger is the increase in the velocity of your life. You are moving through life at a certain speed. It is very similar to driving a car. If you have been driving on neighborhood streets at 35 mph for most of your life, you will be quite used to that velocity and can drive it very safely. If you suddenly get on an interstate and start driving 75 mph, the risks of accident increase dramatically.

Eventually, your awareness will get used to this new speed and you will be able to drive it comfortably and safely. After you have gotten used to driving 75 mph, the change in your mental velocity can be witnessed by the feeling you get when you get off the interstate and start driving 35 mph again. It will feel extremely slooooooowwww, yet it is the same speed that seemed normal for most of your life.

This principle is true for your awareness as well. You have been accustomed to moving through life at a certain speed. Most people exist in a familiar routine. Life lessons may come up, but not on a regular basis. If a person learns one or two major Life lessons per lifetime, they are with the majority. As you practice this technique, your life velocity will accelerate. Life lessons will begin to come at you more quickly, monthly, weekly, even daily. Ideas and perceptions once considered immutable will be called into question. As layers of programming are stripped away, moving ever closer to the true You, you will change and change and change again.

Until becoming acclimated to it, this continual change can be overwhelming. I can't tell you how often people who scoffed when I advised them to limit their practice to seven repetitions per day later returned to me in total chaos because their egos persuaded them to do more and their lives were breaking down.

The technique is extremely powerful. Have patience. Don't let your ego run away with you. In actuality, if you are not meditating, you are probably moving through life at a metaphorical pace that is closer to 5 mph. The technique I am going to share will accelerate your progress.

Ultimately, as you progress to even more powerful techniques, you can go faster than the speed of light and explore the Cosmos if that is your will. Relax. You are on the right track. It will come. You have to learn to drive a car, then fly an airplane before you can move on to the Starship Enterprise. Start practicing this technique and you'll find yourself in Starfleet Academy!

The final danger is to the energy circuits themselves. These circuits are very similar to electrical wires in that they conduct energy. Like electrical wires, if you overload them with energy, they will burn out. The emotional debris within your energy circuits act as resistance. As with electricity, resistance causes heat which can also cause burn out.

Unlike electrical wires, your energy circuits can grow stronger with use, just as your muscles do from working out. As you practice the meditation technique, your circuits will grow stronger and the debris will be cleansed from your system, reducing resistance and allowing you to conduct ever higher amounts of energy.

If you take the time to develop your capacity, you will eventually find yourself, without any more thought or effort than you give to breathing, conducting amounts of energy that would burn out dozens of beginners. Slow and steady wins the race. If you conduct yourself with a little wisdom now, you will find a future beyond any that you imagined.

THE PRACTICE

The Transformation Breath: I will not share the entire technique in this book. I will not even name it. If you are moved to know more about the full technique, you can begin a study and practice of internal alchemy or you can attend a seminar in which it is taught directly. For now, we will call it the Transformation Breath, for that is the effect it will have on your being. Prior to teaching the technique, a few terms need to be introduced to facilitate comprehension.

Energy: Modern science has long since verified that everything is composed of energy and is in constant motion. It has also shown that our bodies and beings are surrounded by and interpenetrated by energy fields. This is no longer a matter for discussion or debate.

Even though matter is seemingly solid, we all know that it is composed of atoms. These atoms are composed of tiny particles spinning around other tiny particles. It is energy that holds these particles together and that bonds the atoms to one another. There is so much energy in these tiny atoms that nuclear explosions result from splitting them.

Just like our solar system, these atoms are composed more of space than of matter. Imagine two solar systems intersecting and passing through one another. The chance of a planet from one making contact with a planet from the other is minuscule. The same is true when 'solid' matter comes together. The chances of the solid parts of one atom touching the solid parts of another are minute.

Energy fields are what stop your hand from passing through a wall when you lean on it, or stop your hands from passing through each other when you applaud. The solidity of matter is an illusion. All is composed of interacting energy fields.

In this meditation technique, we will use consciousness and intent to guide the life force energy. This energy has been called 'The Energy of a Thousand Names.' In various cultures including our own, it has been called chi, ki, prana, manna, the Holy Ghost, kundalini, shakti, the Force and orgone.

Quantum physics has proven that consciousness and intent affect this energy. Since everything is composed of energy, focused intent can have a powerful influence on the material world. Consciously focused intent is the secret of the power of prayer, creative visualization and other means of using awareness to affect reality.

Root Lock: There is a technique common to many mystical systems that has remained hidden from the general public for many years. It has come to public light in recent years, but is still not common knowledge. This technique is called the root lock, so called because it is done at the base, or root, of your being. As with a plant, the root is where energy enters from the Earth.

The root lock is simply a gentle squeeze of the anal sphincter muscle. As with so many simple things, it has powerful effects. Squeezing the anal sphincter muscle creates a hydraulic pressure that promotes circulation of the cerebrospinal fluid. As the Transformation Breath charges this fluid with life force energy, the brain is bathed in charged cerebrospinal fluid. This facilitates the activation of the dormant neurons and higher brain centers.

The root lock also prevents loss of energy. It creates the effect of a one way valve. Energy from the Earth can enter, but it will not escape until the lock is released. Root lock strengthens the pubo-coccygeus muscle. This reduces the effects of urinary incontinence, helps control premature ejaculation and has a number of other beneficial physical effects.

The root lock also generates life force energy and sexual life force. I usually have students begin with a daily practice of 300 repetitions of the root lock. These are gentle squeezes held for a second or so, then released. Do not squeeze so hard that you give yourself hemorrhoids. Be gentle.

Since it doesn't require a lot of focus, I recommend practicing while driving, reading or watching TV. The repetitions can be broken down into blocks of 50 or 100 until enough strength has been developed to do them in a single set. Then, the number can be increased as desired by the practitioner.

The Tongue Switch: The tongue is an energetic switching mechanism. Just as a railroad switch is used to direct trains onto particular tracks, the tongue directs energy into different circuits.

Placing the tip of the tongue on the front of the hard palate by the front teeth directs the energy into the main channel running down the front of the body. Placing the tip of the tongue on the back of the hard palate close to where it meets the soft palate directs the energy up to the Crown via the third ventricle of the brain.

Placing the tip of the tongue on the soft palate as far back as can be reached directs the energy to the hair swirl. In various cultures, the hair swirl and the area just above it outside the body have been known by such terms as bindu, the moon chakra, the Doorway of the Soul and the driver's seat. This third position is the one we will use in the Transformation Breath.

Breath: Breath is the carrier wave of life force energy. Conscious intent combined with breath can guide energy wherever you choose. There is an old adage, "Where thought goes, energy flows." By putting awareness on any location, inside or outside of the body, energy automatically goes there.

Adding breath to the focus greatly magnifies the effect. There are other enhancements, but this is the foundation of the conscious regulation of the life force energy. It can be used for spiritual growth, emotional development, physical healing and martial arts applications.

<u>Relaxation</u>: Relaxation is the most important factor for the success of any meditation practice. Just as squeezing a garden hose reduces the flow of water, so physical, emotional, mental and spiritual tension constrict the flow of life force energy. Relaxation allows the energy to flow and transformation to take place.

I have always said the first, second and third rules of working with the life force are relax, relax, and relax. My mentor in Sound Current meditation said that relaxation is nine times more important than any technique. I don't know how he arrived at that metric, but I agree completely with the point.

<u>The Technique</u>: In the Transformation Breath, we will combine root lock, the tongue switch, breath and focused intent to guide the life force energy. Sit in a relaxed pose with eyes closed and the spine straight. The Transformation Breath is just as effective done in a chair as sitting in the Lotus posture, so don't be concerned with any preconceived notions of meditation poses.

• Apply the root lock.

• Simultaneously place the tip of your tongue on the soft palate.

• Put your attention in the Earth beneath you.

• Begin a long, slow, soft inhalation through your mouth, filling your lungs completely.

• While inhaling, use visualization, intent, focus and breath to draw energy up from the Earth, through the perineum and up the spine to the medulla. From the medulla, bring the energy directly across the brain to the point between your eyebrows. This spot is popularly known as the Third Eye.

• Your inhalation should end as the energy reaches the Third Eye and fills the brain.

- Maintaining your eyelids closed, turn your eyes so you are 'looking' at your Third Eye.

- Maintain your focus there for as long as it is comfortable to hold your breath.

- When you feel the need to exhale, take a sip of air through the nose.

- Simultaneously, release the root lock and the tongue switch.

- Begin a long, slow, controlled exhalation through your mouth while using your focus, intent and visualization to bring energy from the Cosmos in through the Third Eye, into the brain, down the spine, out the perineum and back to the Earth. The exhalation should end as the energy reaches the Earth.

- This is one repetition of the Transformation Breath.

Your breathing should be relaxed, even and regulated. The pause between inhalation and exhalation should be held only as long as is comfortable. Starving yourself of oxygen would be counter productive. Over time, your lung capacity and the length of the pause will increase.

The sip of air at the end of the pause and just prior to exhalation fools the body into thinking it just finished an inhalation. This makes it easier to exhale in a relaxed, regulated manner.

Recommended Practice: My recommendation is to start with seven repetitions of the Transformation Breath each day for a month. It would be ideal if you have some time to sit in stillness after the breathing is complete. But, it is the breathing that is most important at this stage.

If you don't have time to sit in meditation, at least do the seven repetitions of the breath. I tell aspirants that if they really are pressed for time, they can do their breaths while they are using the bathroom. If personal growth is a priority, there is no excuse for missing your practice. Consistency and persistence are great assets.

If you do miss a day, don't get down on yourself. Don't try to 'double up' the next day, either. Just do your breaths as normal as if you never missed.

Seven repetitions may not seem like much, particularly if you are an experienced meditator. It is plenty. Imagine trying to push your car. If you push it slowly and steadily, it will overcome inertia, begin to roll, then gather speed and momentum. If you take a running start and bang into it your car in an attempt to gain instant results, you will end up hurting yourself.

Don't expect whiz bang, lights out epiphanies after the first repetition either. Allow the energy to build. The experiences will come and so will the changes. It is best to go into the practice without any expectations. Having expectations can limit your possibilities to the expected and lead to disappointment if the expectations are not met.

Have only the expectations of an explorer. Keep your mind open and observe what is actually there as you explore your personal landscape. It is a good idea to keep a journal during this phase. Chronicle any experiences you have in your meditations as well as general and specific experiences in your daily life. It is also beneficial to record your dreams.

Many changes are very subtle and go unnoticed as they happen or are quickly forgotten as day to day life asserts itself. Much growth is cumulative rather than happening in bursts. It is similar to not noticing a child's growth on a daily basis, but seeing a photo taken several months prior makes the cumulative change obvious.

Keeping a record will allow you to see the changes that occur over time that would otherwise have gone unnoticed. It will also bring your personal growth into the realm of science, allowing you to draw conclusions from your observations.

The Science of Spirituality: There is no animosity between true science and true spirituality. That dispute has been manufactured as a distraction and a control mechanism. Science is exploration through the use of the scientific method: hypothesis, experiment, observation and conclusion. It can be applied to spiritual exploration with the same validity as the exploration of space and laboratory experiments.

- Hypothesis: If I practice the Transformation Breath daily for a specific period of time, certain changes will occur in my emotional body and higher brain function and translate to my perspective and outlook on life.

- Experiment: I practice the Transformation Breath daily for one year on the schedule set forth in *Blueprint for a Golden Society*.

- Observation: I keep comprehensive notes recording the experiences of my daily meditation practice, my general thoughts and feelings throughout the day, any major events that take place in my life, any shifts in thinking and new realizations that take place.

- Conclusion: At the end of one year, after thorough examination of my notes, careful self-observation and comparison with my past way of being, I can draw conclusions concerning the efficacy of practice of the Transformation Breath.

Thus, the Scientific Method can equally be applied to spiritual and personal growth, allowing a true exploration and understanding of our individual and collective Nature.

Recommended Further Practice: As you practice seven daily repetitions of the Transformation Breath, observe to see if your life becomes more chaotic. If events are too overwhelming, reduce the number of breaths. If all seems well at the end of one month, increase to 14 daily repetitions for the next month. Continue to observe yourself. If there is too much chaos, decrease to seven daily repetitions. If all is well at the end of the second month, increase to 21 repetitions.

After another month, repeat the self-analysis. If you feel ready, increase to 28. If not, hold steady at 21 or decrease as needed. The goal is to find the proper balance for YOU. You want to do enough repetitions that velocity, change and life lessons increase without getting to the point that you are in continuous chaos. There should be a balance. Most people find that the following cycle occurs.

Change stirs things up and confronts us with difficulties. As we work through the difficulties, learn the available lessons and integrate the changes, we reach a plateau of peace and relaxation. After a time, more difficulties arise and we are confronted with more challenges and lessons. After processing them, another plateau is reached.

The trick is to find the right balance between change and stillness. Too much change and we have unrelieved chaos. Too little change and we fall into stagnation. Each of us is different and we have to find our own place of balance. There are no set rules.

The goal is to drive your vehicle as fast as you safely can. You want to constantly push the envelope without pushing past your capacity. It is ok to cross over the lines on the road every now and again, but you don't want to crash into walls, trees or other cars, damaging your vehicle or harming other drivers.

Find the number of breaths that works for you. As you grow so accustomed to a new velocity that it becomes your new baseline, you will be able to increase the number of breaths to reach an even higher level. Follow the schedule. Give yourself time to adjust to increased repetitions.

Avoid comparing yourself to others and to the number of repetitions they are doing. We are all different. More repetitions do not necessarily equate to higher levels of evolution. It might even mean the contrary. One person may be far more dense than another and require more repetitions to achieve the same effect. It may be that one person requires 28 repetitions to get the same results as someone who needs only seven.

Don't let ego run away with you. Focus on yourself. Keep your nose out of the affairs of others. Remember, your job is to focus on your light bulb. Leave others to focus on theirs.

After attaining to 28 repetitions, you can split the daily meditation into two sets or do one long set. By this time, you should have developed an increased capacity to sustain energy. I will leave adding more repetitions to your judgement. I do advise waiting at least two months between each incremental addition of seven repetitions. Give your physical and energetic bodies time to adjust.

A BROADER VIEW OF CREATION

<u>He Went to Paris</u>: Do not think for one instant that I am presenting the Transformation Breath as the Be-All, Do-All of spiritual awareness. Far from it. It is only a step, a vital step nonetheless, of your overall personal growth and development.

In essence, I am teaching you arithmetic so that in the future you can learn trigonometry and calculus. That may not seem much to some people, but in a world where the establishment doesn't acknowledge the existence of mathematics, learning arithmetic is a huge evolutionary step.

I want to leave you with a broader view of Creation. Hopefully, this will help you gain a different perspective of your individual relationship to the Whole, and will also better show how a Golden Society fits in to the larger picture. Do NOT believe anything I say. Anyone who asks you to believe them is selling you something.

Always maintain an open, but skeptical mind. Creation is amazing in its infinite variety. Remain open to all possibilities, but insist on proof. If someone tells you that they know how things are, insist that they share with you a means of experiencing it and knowing if for yourself. If they tell you to believe them, go the other way.

I know Paris is there. I've been there. I can tell you about Paris, but you can never know for certain until you see it for yourself. Based on what you know of me, you can assess the probability of the reliability of what I tell you about Paris. But, until you experience it for yourself, you will never be absolutely certain.

The same is true for spiritual experiences. Other people can tell you about them. You can weigh the probability of what they say based on their past reliability, what you know about their character and a range of other factors. Yet, you cannot truly know the veracity of their statements until you experience the truth for yourself.

With spiritual experience, as with a trip to Paris, I can tell you how I got there. I can also tell you of other routes that I know and stories of how others have reached the goal, but there are always more ways to get there. You must decide for yourself the route that works best for you. It may be by following a path well worn by those who have gone before and it may be via a new trail that you blaze. The point is that you get there, have your own experience and draw your own conclusions.

Even though it is the same city, your experience of Paris will be different from mine. We may both see the Eiffel Tower, the Arc de Triomphe, the Louvre and other landmarks, but the overall experience will be unique to each of us. The weather will be different. You will meet different people than I. The political and economic climate will have changed. The harvest will be different. Those and a host of other variables will be distinct.

Even more significantly, your experience will be sensed and interpreted though different cultural, emotional and personal history matrices than mine. Though we will have experience of the same city, our experiences will be totally unique to each of us.

This analogy especially holds true for spiritual experience. There are certain constants that mark each experience, but there are also differences that make each unique to the individual observer. It is our privilege, right and duty to explore Creation on our own. Each person is in a different place in their individual exploration. Know that your experiences are just as legitimate as those of any others. Don't let anyone or anything invalidate who you are, where you have been or where you are going.

If anyone asks you to believe something, ask them to give you a way to experience it for yourself. If they can't, go the other way. They are looking to control you for their own benefit. So, once again, do NOT believe anything that I say. I offer the Transformation Breath as an initial means of experiencing and verifying for yourself.

The Skyscraper Made of Sound: Metaphor has to be used to describe Creation, because our temporal minds are too limited to grasp the actuality. My favorite metaphor is a 90 story building with a 90 story basement. This hard level in which we live is the ground floor. The 90th level is the Crown Chakra of the Cosmos. The journey of your eternal Life is to the 90th level of the building. Passing through the Crown of the Cosmos is graduation from the School of Life and a whole new existence begins.

The idea that Creation is composed of and Created through Sound may seem strange to so many people who are raised on the idea of Divine Light. It was to me as well. I can remember when I attained to the highest levels available through Light Body Yoga. My mentor started pushing me with the concept of Sound. "Why do you want to focus on the Light," he would ask, "when it is the Sound that Creates the Light?"

My initial response was, "Leave me the hell alone!" I had put so much effort and energy into getting to where I had at a much younger age than I expected to get there that I just wanted to be left alone to rest for a while. Sooner rather than later, a disquiet came upon me. Remaining still for any longer would have led to stagnation. I asked for more, and the Sound Current opened a whole new world to me. It was the final missing piece of the puzzle and everything clicked into place.

Knowledge of the Sound Current is embedded in nearly every religion and mystical system, though virtually all have lost awareness of that knowledge. "In the beginning was the Word, and the Word was God and the Word was with God." So begins Genesis, and with an understanding of the Sound Current, entirely new interpretations come forth.

The Sound Current is referenced historically as the Word, the Logos, the Song of Songs, the Music of the Spheres, the Aum, the Amoun, the Amen and more. They all refer to the primal Sound of Creation.

Modern science confirms that sound is the source of creation. Scientific articles state that the universe is a hologram and there are three sources of sound that create that hologram. This is modern verification of an ancient truth.

Religious persecution forced Sound Current teachings into hiding and eventually the thread was lost to most cultures. The Masons entreat their initiates to 'Go forth and seek the lost Word." With all due respect to Dan Brown, whose novel, *The Lost Symbol*, is an exciting adventure read and romp through American history, the Lost Word/Symbol is the Sound Current. I believe the Masons have lost this thread as well and the ritual has become empty.

Awareness of the Sound Current empowers individuals to spiritual independence. It had to be crushed at any cost for the plutocrats to achieve a slave state. Awareness of the Sound Current can return the spiritual freedom that is our inheritance.

Sound Current meditation allows the practitioner to travel up the stream toward the Source of Creation. As you proceed up the levels, you will encounter spiritual beings. They are part of the Hierarchy of Creation and have been referred to as angels, gods, lords of light, divine beings and many other names. It doesn't matter how you reference them.

If you have developed enough of a sense of Self, they will meet you as equals and be willing to teach you. But, if you try to worship them, the floor will open beneath you and you won't be allowed back until you grow beyond that.

Worship causes great disruption on the higher levels of Creation and is allowed only on the lower levels. Worship is reserved for the spiritually immature, those who have not developed a sense of Self and an awareness of the Divinity within. As such, these people need to look outside themselves for guidance, instruction and focus. There is a certain place in Creation beyond which worship is not accepted. The higher levels of Creation are reserved for the independent and Self-aware.

No true spiritual teacher ever wanted to be worshipped. The religions that tell you to do so are a lie. The desire of true spiritual teachers is to free humanity from spiritual bondage. Their message is that each person can accomplish everything the teacher has accomplished, and more. Sound Current meditation is the means to do that. For this reason, it has been ruthlessly suppressed by the slave forces.

Each of us is born an independent being. The ultimate goal for each of us is to pass through the One Light, the Crown Chakra of Creation, and graduate from the School of Life. Approximately half way between this Earth level and the Crown are several levels composed of self-luminous Golden Light.

Two members of the Cosmic Hierarchy are in charge of these levels. One is responsible for the Lower Eternal Golden Realms. The other is responsible for the Upper Eternal Golden Realms.

The experience in these realms is Love and peace. Many aspirants attain to these levels, experience this Universal Love, and assume they have reached Heaven and the end of their journey. This is a trap, a sweet, comfortable trap. Thinking they have reached the end, these aspirants never seek beyond.

Standing before the throne of the Being responsible for the Upper Eternal Golden Realms, if you know to look, there is an exit that takes you to the next level. There you will find the Eternal Silver Realms and the levels beyond those leading to the Crown of Creation, the One Light.

The reason for creating a Golden Society is to empower humanity to attain to the awareness associated with the Eternal Golden Realms, to live in Universal Love with knowledge of the interconnected nature of all of Life and of the inherent Divinity of each human being. Once this has been attained, there will be enough Wisdom in the society for humans to consciously evolve to higher levels of Life of their own accord.

You may wonder, if Sound Current meditation is the means of such fabulous attainments, why I taught you a technique from a Light Body school. I have observed aspirants who went directly to Sound Current meditation, skipping the development that comes with Light Body practice.

Many of these people have attained incredible levels of spiritual awareness and achievement. But, because they have not addressed their emotional development, when they return to their bodies, their earthly existences are often chaotic and dysfunctional since they are still subject to their emotional wounds and fall prey to the traumas they have experienced.

I recommend that aspirants begin with a practice of Light Body meditation to clear and heal the emotional body. There is no such thing as perfecting the emotions, but they can be developed to a point that they no longer control one's actions or sabotage one's decisions. After a certain level of emotional healing and maturity have been achieved, I recommend moving on to Sound Current practice, provided that is the calling of your heart.

Always keep in mind that the purpose of Life is to Be YourSelf. To do that, you must use your heart as your guide. The Joy in your heart is who you are. It will guide you to the lessons that Life holds for you. Steer your life and make your decisions from the causal place above your emotions, but let your heart be your compass and your GPS.

If your heart tells you to be a sculptor, let the causal self decide how to go about it. You will need training, tools, materials, a place to live and food. These plans and decisions are best made causally, but the inspiration must come from the heart.

After some time, you will have garnered all of the Life lessons that sculpting can bring and it will no longer be fulfilling. Your heart will guide you to the next place. Perhaps as a healer you will find your next lessons and growth. Whatever it is that your heart tells you, rise to the causal to make your plans.

Thus you will progress though Life, learning, growing, then moving on when necessary. At some point, though, for some people, there will be nothing left on this level that appeals to your heart and your fulfillment. No career will draw you. No vocation will attract you. The world will seem a little empty and flat.

That is a sign that you have learned the lessons that this level has to offer. The time has come to proceed vertically. Sound Current meditation is the means to that end. When it is time for you to seek a Sound Current school, I highly recommend you seek a school of the Right Hand Path.

I will not go into deep explanations of the other paths. Suffice it to say that the Right Hand Path is for independent individuals who are ready to take responsibility for themselves and their place in this majestic, sublime Creation. They have a highly developed sense of Self, are beyond worship and are ready to learn higher lessons and to take their places in the Cosmic Hierarchy or to pass through the Crown, graduate from the School of Life and move on to another realm of existence.

THE CROSSROADS

My friends, humanity is at a momentous crossroads. With courage and Love, we can move into a glorious future beyond what our temporal minds can imagine. I have done my best to provide a blueprint and a map. It is up to us collectively and individually to manifest our Golden Future.

I will leave you with one final gift. Go to some place quiet or plug your ears. Listen. That ringing sound in your ears is *your* tone, your unique portion of the Divine Symphony, the Cosmic Sound Current. It is your ***direct*** connection to the Divine Creator. No one stands between you and God. Use this knowledge with Wisdom.

I wish Love, Peace, Joy, Fulfillment and a Golden Future for each of you.

AUTHOR'S NOTE

After fighting an inspiring battle, my mother passed away on May 1, 2012, finally succumbing to the ravages of cancer after expending every bit of her financial and personal resources. Her death was beautiful. Having lovingly said goodbye to family and friends, she passed peacefully in my company. In addition to showing to me first hand the effects of the dysfunctional business side of the medical industry, her final gift to me was a magnificent demonstration of inner strength and personal courage. It has been a privilege to assist her through this process.

To the many doctors, nurses and other health care professionals who treated her with so much courtesy, compassion and professionalism, I extend my eternal gratitude and respect. I feel and understand your frustration at having your hands tied by the government-corporate medical complex.

Special thanks go to the hospice nurses, assistants and administrators serving Montrose, CO. Particular thanks to Gloria, Derek, Debbie, Daisy, Julie and Julie, and all of the others who assisted my mother and me through her dying process with such compassion, care, professionalism and humor. Every day, Hospice demonstrates clearly that non-profit wellness care can be efficient, effective, professional and compassionate.

My wish is that this book inspires the co-creation of a better world for my mother and for all human souls to incarnate in the future. May she come back to a world of Joy, Love, Peace, Fulfillment and Growth. I love you, Mom. You will always be in my heart. Thank you.

14116181R00111

Made in the USA
Charleston, SC
22 August 2012